THE
TRIBAL CODE

THE TRIBAL CODE

Timeless lessons in survival and success

Jo Owen

Auvian Press

CONTENTS

Introduction   7

1 The leadership code   11
Act the part   13
Take responsibility   15
Make a difference   17
Show courage: step up, not back   19
Leading from the front   21
Leadership is a contact sport   23
Learn the code   25

2 The team code   33
Respect your tribe   35
One for all and all for one   37
Survival is a collective effort   43
Communicate less, understand more   45
Trust the messenger, not the message   49
Make technology your servant, not your master   51

3 The change code   55
Change or die   57
Migrate to greener pastures   63
Control your destiny, or someone else will   65

4 The strategy code   71
Seek fit, not perfection   75
Focus, focus, focus   85

Unfair fights are the best fights	90
Defend what you have	97
Embrace risk	99
Escape the prison of success	101
Escape the resource trap	103

5 The cultural code — 109
Respect for the community	111
Earn respect	113
Celebrate to survive	121

6 The ancestral code — 127
Appreciate the invisible: the rule of law	129
Education, education, education	131
Help from the invisible hand	133
Enjoy your freedom	137

7 Your personal code — 141
Build your know-how	145
Count your blessings	153
How to wake up in the morning	155
Know what you want	157

About the book	161
About the author	162

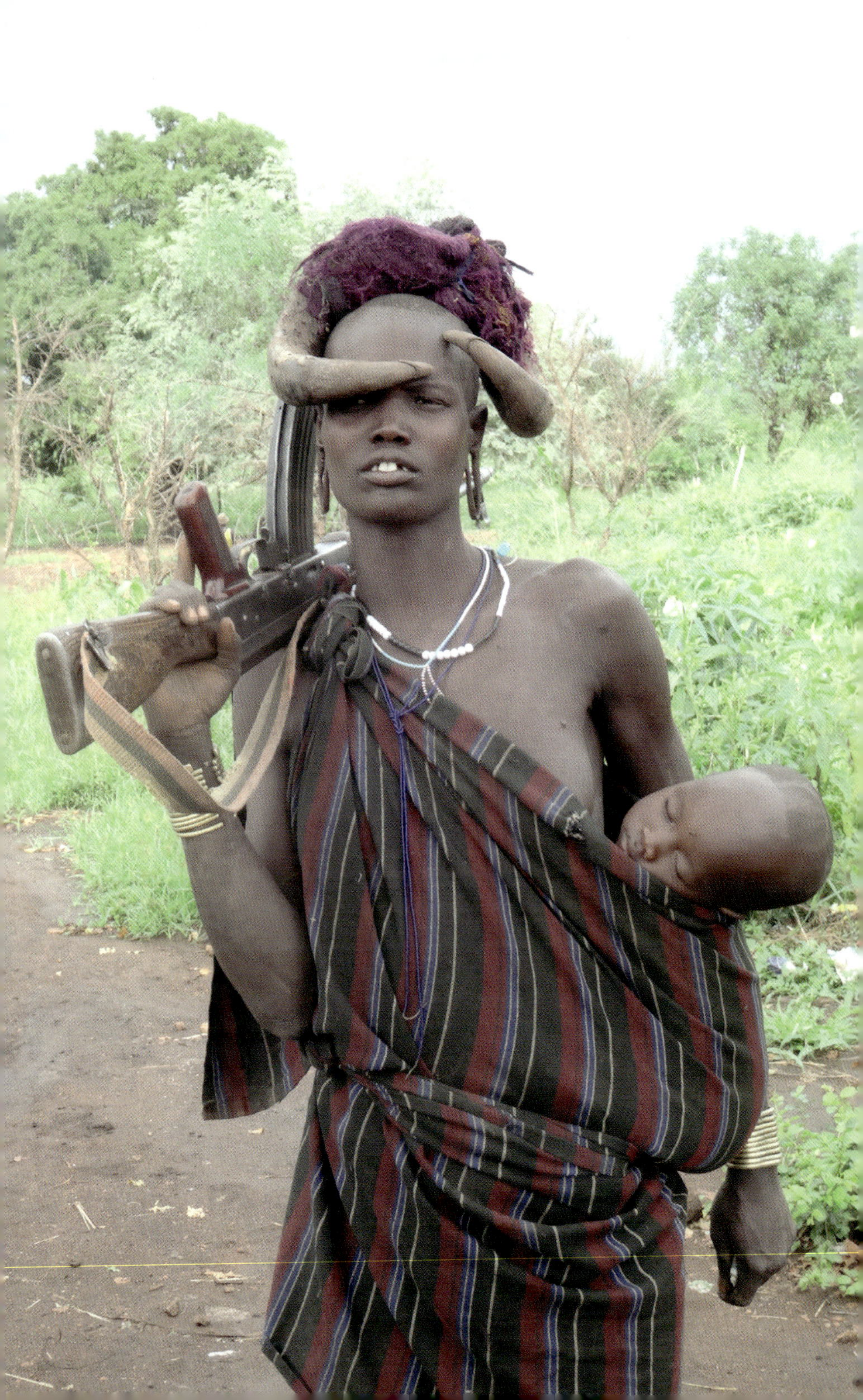

Introduction

The art of survival

Tribes have survived far longer, with far fewer resources in far harsher environments than most modern firms. So maybe, just maybe, we can learn something about survival and success from these great survivors.

Tribes survive longer. On average, firms only survive 7 years in the S&P 500. 57% of the firms in the FTSE 100 have been taken over or overtaken in this millennium. A tribe which survives less than a generation is not a successful tribe.

Tribes survive with fewer resources. Fire your lawyers, consultants, HR specialists, Health and Safety and IT departments. Throw away your mobile phone. Ditch the internet. Make do without your car or coffee maker. Now start leading. Tribal leadership is leadership stripped bare, without all the corporate life support systems which enable us and imprison us.

Tribes survive in far harsher environments. Imagine a world where your competition does not want to beat you: they want to eat you. If you mess up, you will not get fired: you may get shot. Climate change does not mean sunny summers: it means your livestock dies and you starve. Tribes understand survival.

Firms go from good to great to gone, with tedious regularity. Tribes just keep going. We can learn from them.

(left) Hamar mother: determined to survive. South Omo valley.

1
THE LEADERSHIP CODE

Act the part

Take responsibility

Make a difference

Show courage: step up, not back

Leadership is a contact sport

Learn the code

The author attempting to discover the leadership code.
Papua New Guinea. Photo: Anthony Willoughby.

I asked the elders, the warriors, the children, the women, the young and the old the same question: what makes a good leader? They all gave the same answer.

They knew it was not about having feathers in your head dress: leadership is about how you act, not how you look. Leaders act the part in three ways:

> Make a difference

> Take responsibility

> Show courage

Everyone I met seemed to have the same mantra: **courage, contribution** (make a difference) and **responsibility**. It was the same story from the Highlands of Papua New Guinea to the plains of Africa.

For tribes, these values do not exist as logos on brass plaques, motivational posters and tribal videos in their mud huts.

I was soon to discover that these values exist not as words, but as actions. If you want to lead, act the part.

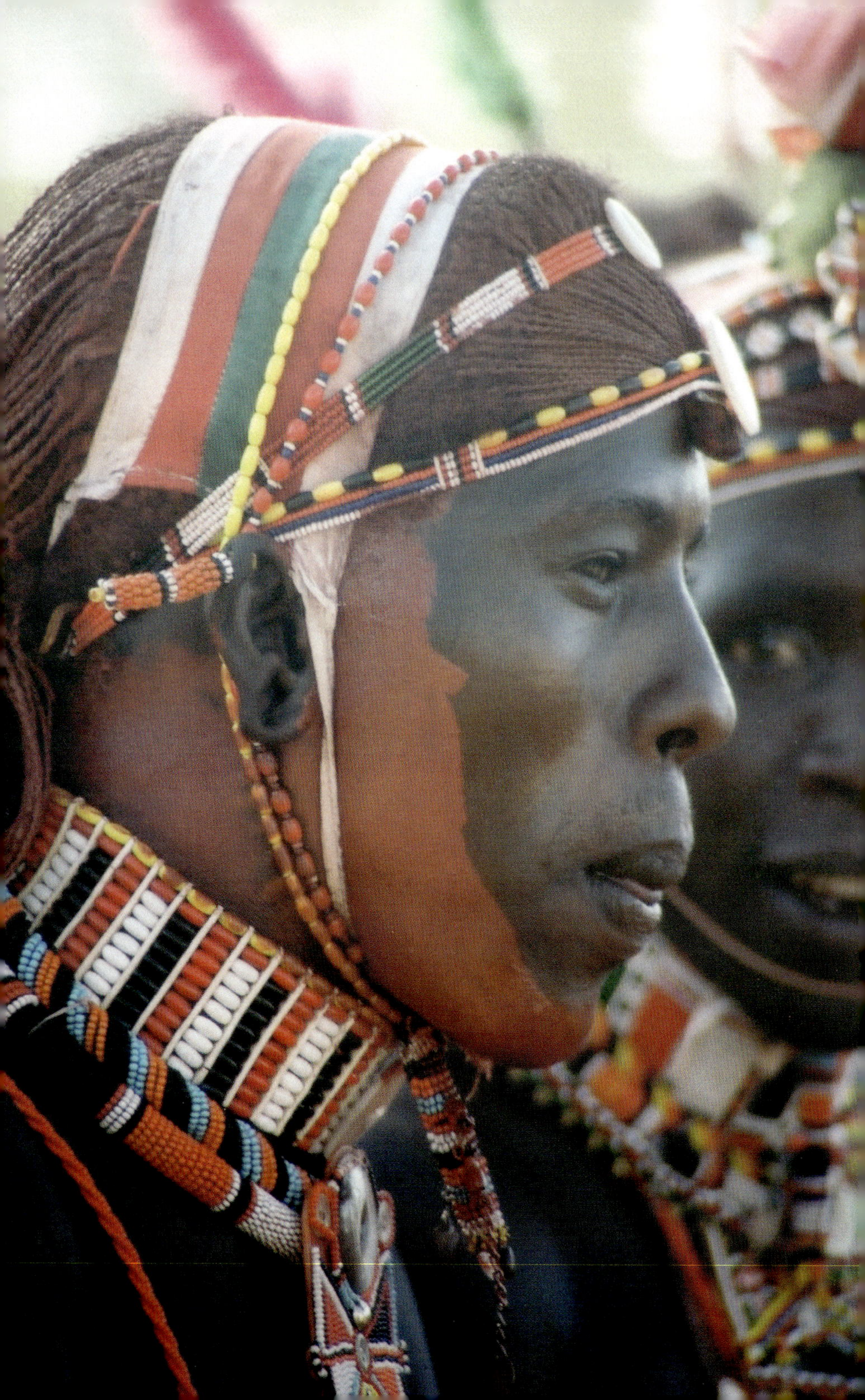

Act the part: be a role model

Chief Daniel decided to teach some budding warriors a lesson.

He led them out on a patrol of their territory. As with all teenagers across the world, the budding warriors messed around. As Daniel went along, he occasionally saw a piece of litter on the ground. He picked it up and tucked it away to dispose of later. The teenagers ignored him.

After a few hours of walking and litter picking, eventually one of the teenagers got the message: sheepishly, he picked up some litter and tucked it away. Daniel smiled and said nothing.

Thereafter, any time the teenagers saw some litter, they raced to see who could pick it up first. Lesson delivered.

You may not remember all the details of your bosses' achievements from five years ago, but will remember vividly what they were like. For better or worse.

You will not be remembered for what you achieve. You will be remembered for how you are. Choose well.

(left) Chief Daniel, Laikipia. Leadership is not just how you look, but how you act.

THE TRIBAL CODE

Choidog. Mongolian Living National Treasure and champion horse trainer. At home on the Steppe.

Take responsibility

At age 74, Choidog was the sports superstar of Mongolia. In a horse mad country, he was the top horse trainer. A nadaam (festival) was set up in the Steppe to celebrate him becoming a Living National Treasure. The centre piece was a 10km horse race for 60 horses, with a motor bike as the winning prize.

The race was a stitch up. Choidog's horse was meant to win. But half way in, disaster struck: the saddle came loose and the jockey had to dismount to fix it. He still nearly won, but nearly does not get the motorbike.

How would you react when you miss the big prize on your big day?

Choidog laughed and said: "That shows how much more I have to learn!" The festivities flowed again.

Taking responsibility for successes is easy. Taking responsibility for setbacks is harder, but liberates the team. Taking responsibility for your own feelings is hardest of all. If you are angry, annoyed and cynical those are your choices which affect your whole team.

You can choose how you feel. Choose well.

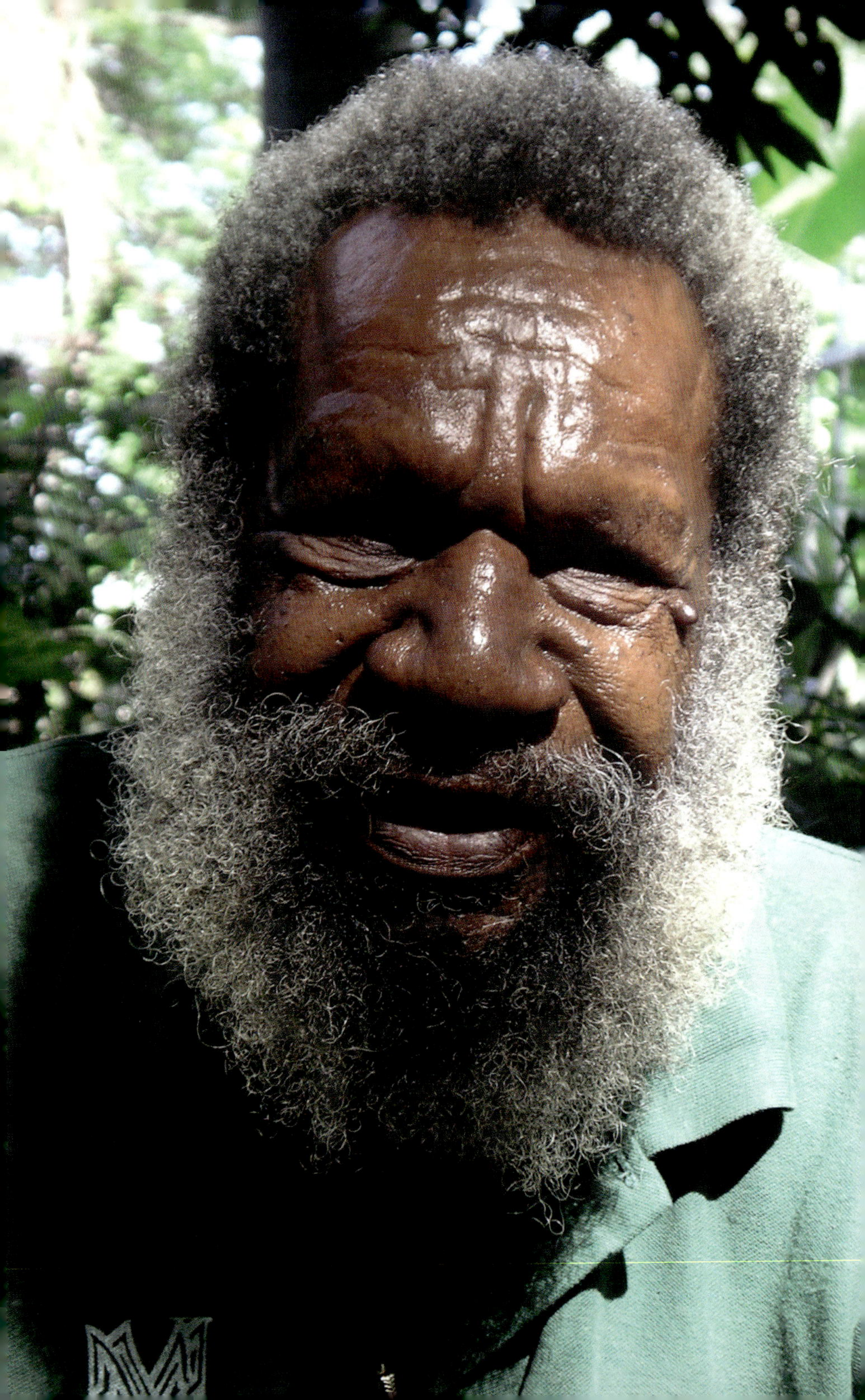

Make a difference: wells, wars and the moment of truth

Sir Joseph Nomburi liked to claim that he had be born in the Stone Age (in the Highlands of Papua New Guinea) and lived to the space age (as the ambassador to the Imperial Court in Tokyo).

As a young government officer in the Highlands, he often found himself in the middle of tribal conflict, which is endemic in the area. One conflict was about to erupt because a tribesman had been thrown down a well.

Young Joseph persuaded the tribes to halt hostilities, to allow the body to be retrieved. No one wanted to retrieve the body: it was a dangerous and potentially one way trip down the well. Joseph had the power to tell someone to do the work, but he decided to set an example.

He went down, and came back up. The body was not dead: it was dead drunk. He had not been pushed down the well, but had fallen, drunk, into it.

So instead of war, the two tribes had a feast. They stayed well clear of the well.

At that moment, Joseph had acted the part of a true leader:

Make a difference: stop a tribal conflict

Take responsibility: solve the problem

Show courage: going down the well

(left) Sir Joseph Nomburi, at home in Papua New Guinea.

THE TRIBAL CODE

The author making peace with a pack of hyenas. Do not try this at home. Or anywhere else. Photo: Hiromi Takahashi

Show courage: hyenas and the moment of truth

Suddenly, a pack of hyenas came charging straight at us out of some dense bush. What would you do?

I did what any sensible coward would do. I hid behind the warriors, so that they would get killed first and I could run away. The warriors started to laugh in the face of imminent death, which struck me as one reason they were warriors and I was not.

The cause of their laughter became clear a moment later: a small child with a small stick was chasing the hyenas. The child knew from years, generations, of cultural indoctrination that his job was to protect the goats of the village at any cost. In that one moment, the child had become a leader because he acted like a leader:

Make a difference: save the goats from the hyenas

Take responsibility: he did not run for help, he took action

Show courage: the hyenas knew they had met their match

Tribal leaders show the same survival values around the world. Your values are your choice. Values are not about what you say, but about what you do. Be your best.

THE TRIBAL CODE

Leading from the front

We all know that leaders should lead from the front, like Kings of old leading their troops into battle. The last time an English king did that was George II at the Battle of Dettingen in 1743: leading from the front can be risky.

But there is a tribal alternative: lead from the back. On the salt caravan to Timbuktu, the leader of the caravan is at the back, where he can see which loads are shifting and which camels and Tuareg are struggling. And in the Arctic, the Saami follow the herd rather than lead it, so that they can spot and help stragglers more easily.

If everyone knows where they are going, anyone can be at the front. The real job of the leader is not to set the direction, if it is known. The job of the leader is to look after the team and to help it perform to its full potential.

Setting the direction is the easy part of the leader's job. The harder part is helping your team get to where it needs to go.

Opposite, above Tuareg map of their salt caravan to Timbuktu. Note the leader at the back of the caravan (centre row).

Below: Reindeer migration in the Arctic. The Saami follow the herd which knows where to go.

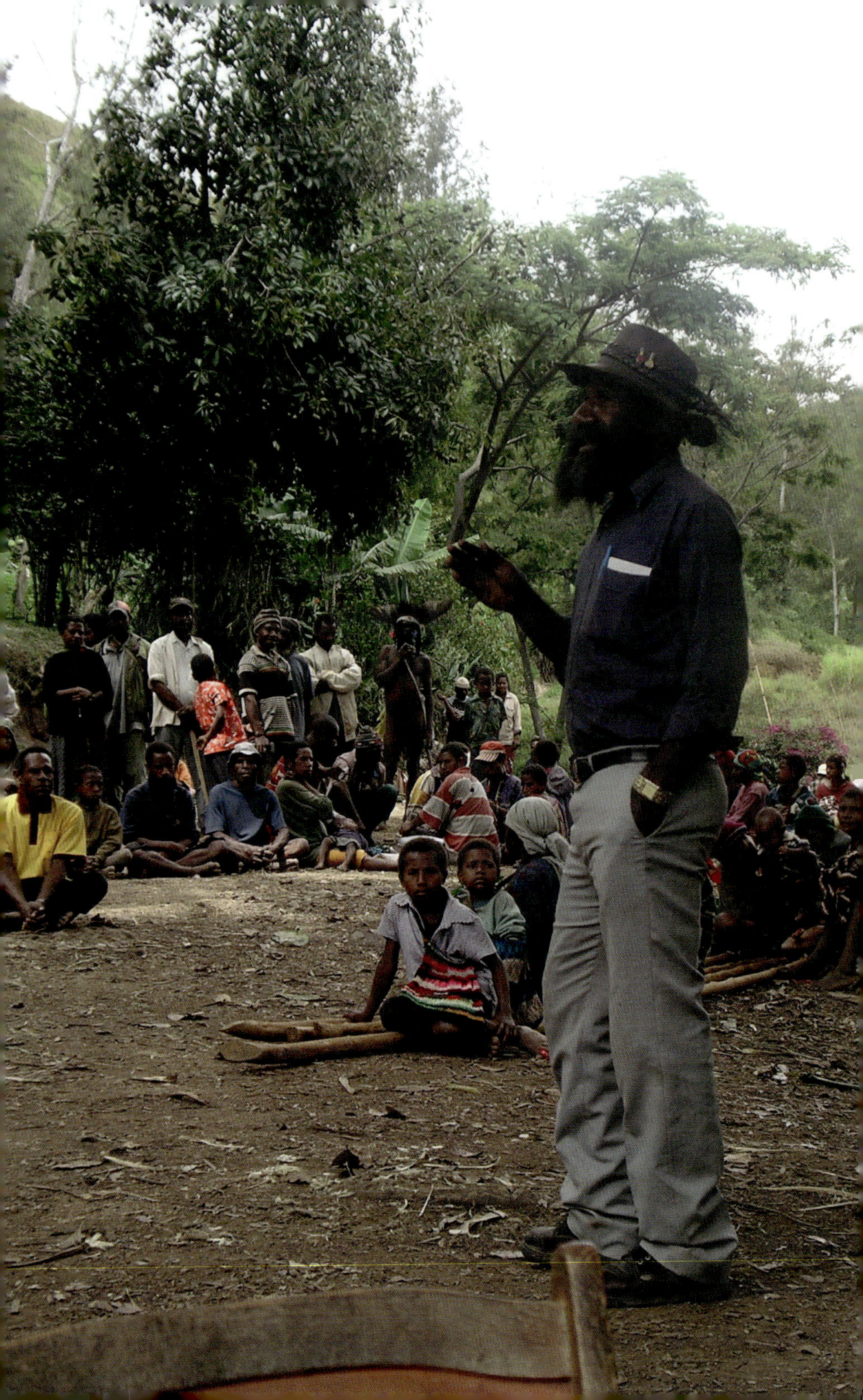

Leadership is a contact sport

By tradition, only missionaries, mercenaries or madmen go into the Highlands of Papua New Guinea. I knew I was not a missionary or mercenary, so I wondered whether the village would really want to accept my presence.

On my arrival, Chief John summoned everyone to a village meeting. They all sat down on the single mud road through the village. One table and a chair were found in different huts and I was invited to sit down behind the table.

Chief John asked the village whether they should greet me (or possibly eat me: I had no way of knowing what they were discussing). It was a lengthy discussion with many questions asked.

Eventually, they decided to feast on a pig, not on me. I was treated as one of theirs and given the best hospitality, and protection, anyone could ask for.

Chief John understood that decisiveness is not just about making the right decision. It is about building commitment. That means not making a decision from behind a desk but with the people who are affected.

Lead through people, not through papers.

(left) Chief John holding a village meeting in the main street. Papua New Guinea.

THE TRIBAL CODE

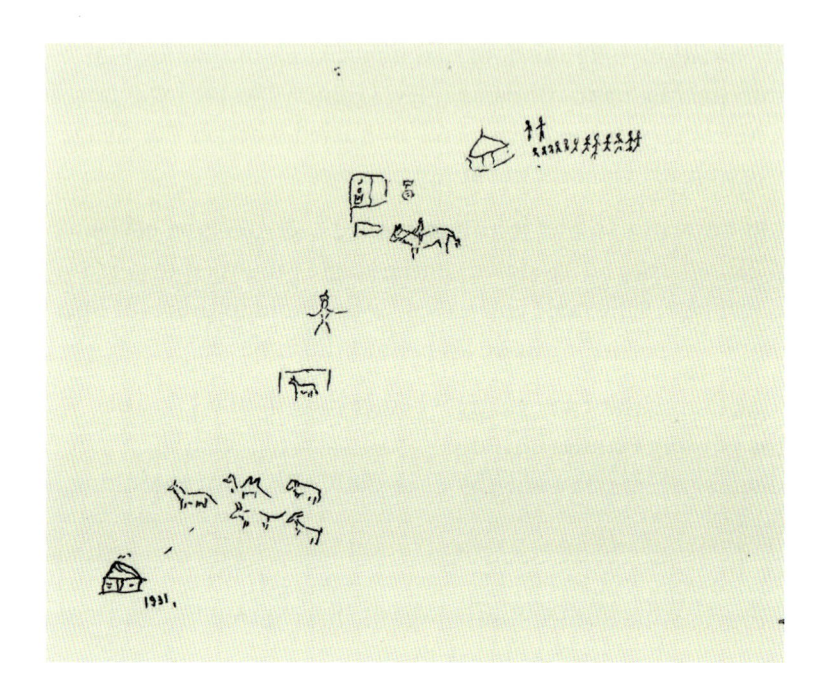

Choidog's life map. Mongolia. All horses and jockeys; no mention of his life as a wrestler and accountant under communist rule.

You only excel at what you enjoy because success takes unrelenting focus, hard work and discretionary effort sustained for decades.

Learn the code: horse sense

Choidog, the champion horse trainer of Mongolia, had a hard life. He based his success on three principles:

Horse sense: you have to excel at your craft, whatever it is. That takes decades of discretionary effort, which only comes if you enjoy what you do. Expertise makes you a boffin: leaders need something more than horse sense.

People sense. Choidog invested hugely in training child jockeys, and in dealing with all the other people who help him find and train the best horses. Every great leader succeeds with and through other people.

Hard work and focus. In the Communist era, Choidog was required to become an implausible mix of accountant and wrestler. But his life map only shows horses and jockeys: even under Communist rule, that is all he cared about: he would do his accounting and wrestling and then focus on his horses. That required huge effort, risk and focus.

Is this the leadership formula which the gurus missed:

Build your horse sense: acquire technical expertise

Build your people sense: make things happen through others

Focus, focus, focus on what you care about and enjoy

Work hard, or hope to get lucky. But hope is not a method and luck is not a strategy.

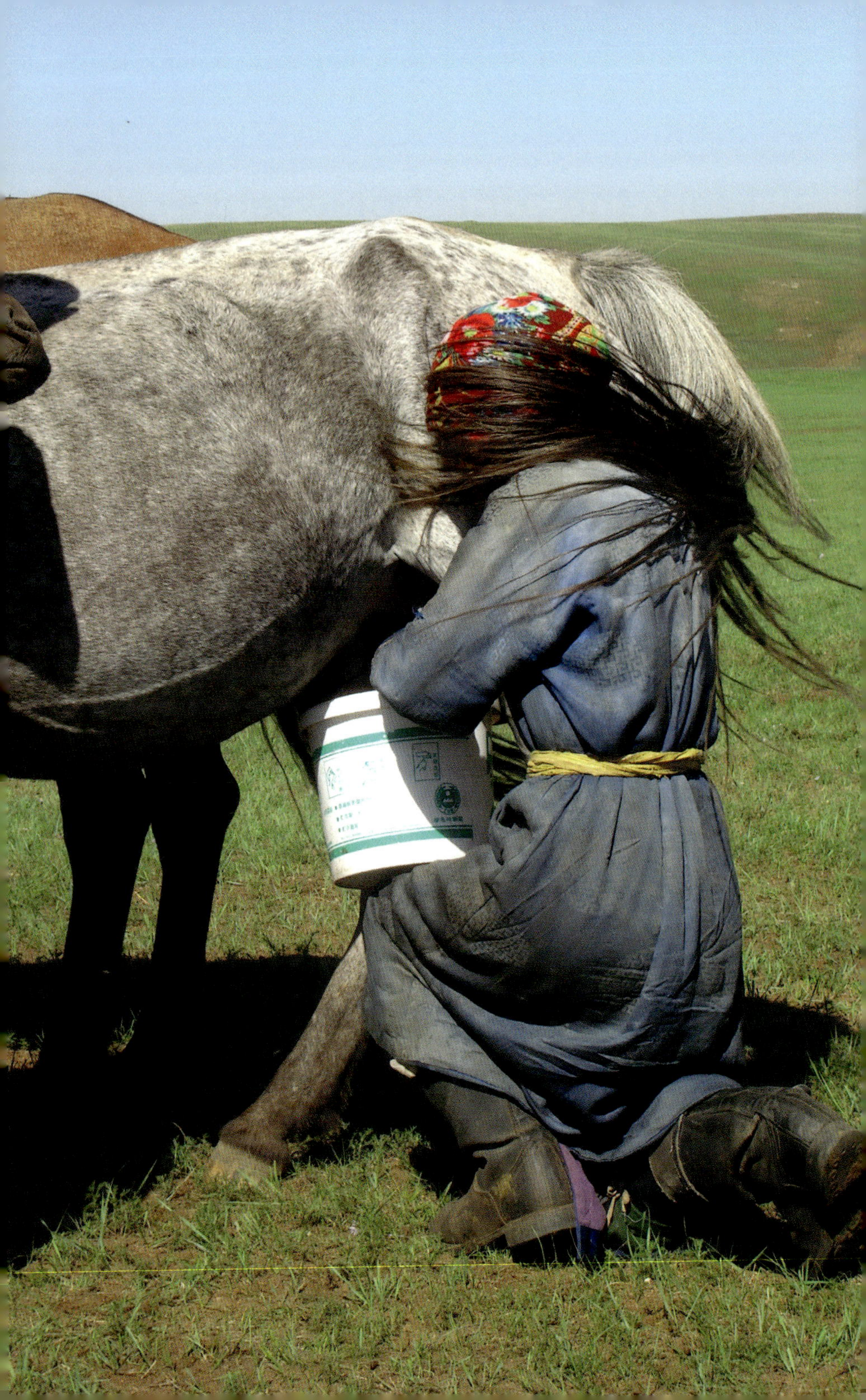

Learn the code: the nomadic training school

Celebrations in Mongolia require drinking fermented mare's milk. Even the nomads admit it is an acquired taste: it is well worth not acquiring.

Milking the mares is tough. Men hold the impatient mare steady, and women milk while the mare swishes its tail. When they find a cooperative mare, a young girl might get the chance to try her hand at milking under close supervision.

In every tribe it was the same: whether it is learning to hunt or make fire, everything is learned through experience, observation and close support from the elders. Nomads reckon that by the age of ten, children should be able to do most of what adults go, except for the heavy lifting.

Nomads understand leadership training:

› Focus on experience not theory
› Coaching, not courses
› Just in time learning
› What works in your context now.

Your next corporate away day will offer better refreshments than fermented mare's milk. But will it have better training?

(left) Milking mares on the Steppe

THE TRIBAL CODE

Learning to make fire, Papua New Guinea

The Bambara Life (Mali) counter clockwise from bottom left: 20 years learning, 20 years doing and 20 years teaching the next generation. Simple.

Learn the code: the school of life

Tribal leaders are an MBA-free zone. So how do they learn to lead? I ask business groups how they learn to lead, and I let them choose two of six options. See which two you pick:

- › Books
- › Courses
- › Role models
- › Bosses
- › Peers
- › Experience

Virtually no one chooses books or courses, which could be bad news for an author who runs courses. Everyone chooses personal experience, or observed experience (bosses, peers and role models). This makes sense: you see something work in your context and repeat it; if something fails you do not repeat that mistake.

We learn leadership the same way tribes learn: it is an apprenticeship model based on experience, not theory. The tribes have the advantage that they know what works in their context.

Learning from experience is dangerous. It is a random walk of good and bad experiences. Books and courses cannot give you the answer, but they can help you make sense on the nonsense you encounter, and help you put structure on your random walk of experience.

Enjoy your journey of discovery, but structure it.

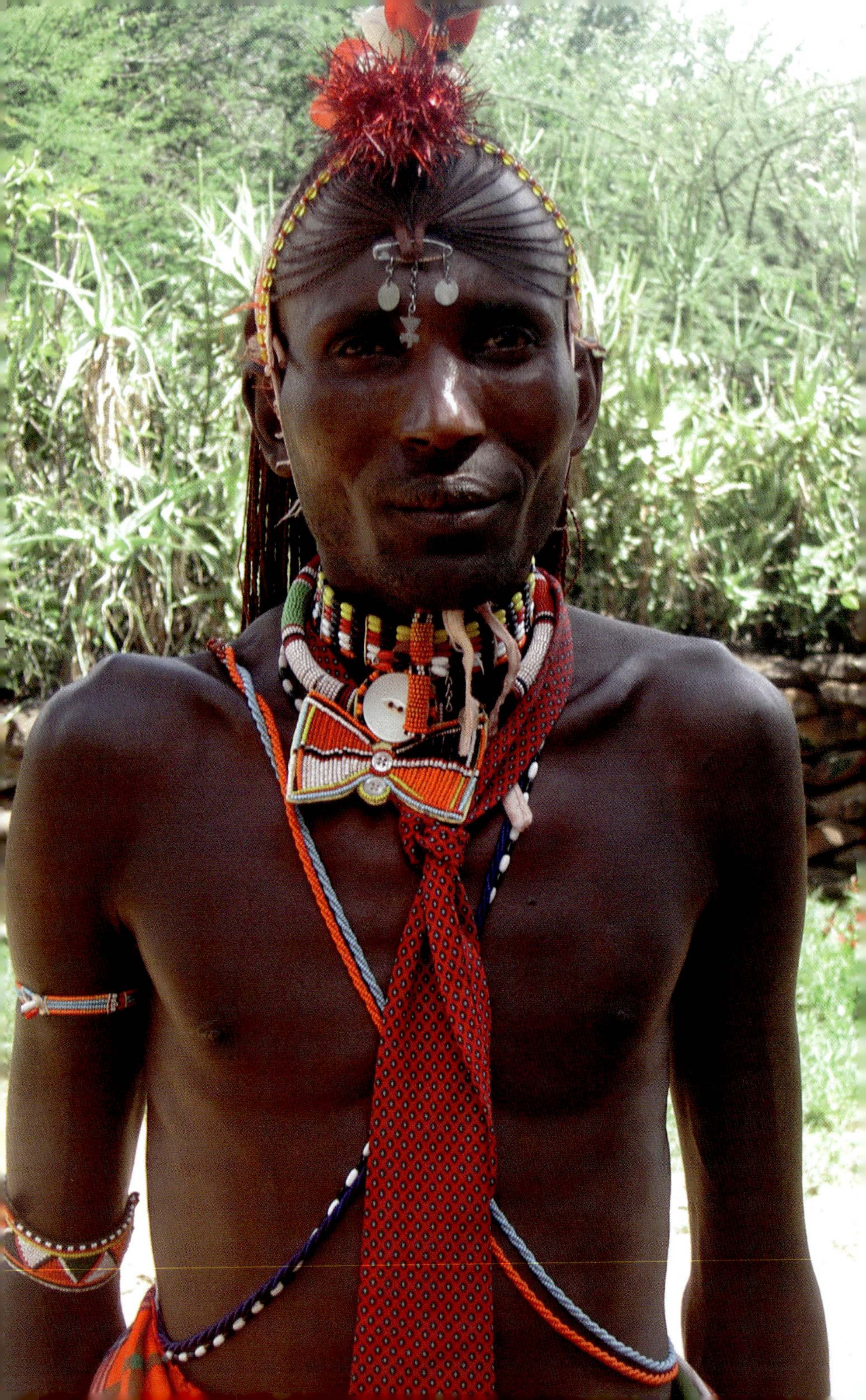

The Leadership Code checklist

1. Leadership is about what you do, not about your title: you can lead at any level.
2. Leaders are remembered for how they are, not just what they do. Choose how you want to be remembered.
3. Values are what you do, not what you say.
4. Leaders need courage for difficult decisions, difficult conversations and taking risks.
5. Leaders are responsible, not just for successes but also for setbacks and how they feel and how they act.
6. Leaders focus on what they can give, not just on what they can take.
7. Leaders need more than technical skills (horse sense): you need people and political skills.
8. Leaders learn from experience, not from theory. Work out what works for you in your context.
9. Leaders never stop learning. When your context changes, you have to change.
10. Success is hard work, so make sure you enjoy what you do.

(left) Chief Kool. Looking dapper in the author's tie.

2
THE TEAM CODE

Respect your tribe

One for all and all for one

Survival is a collective effort

Communicate less, understand more

Trust the messenger, not the message

Make technology your servant, not your master

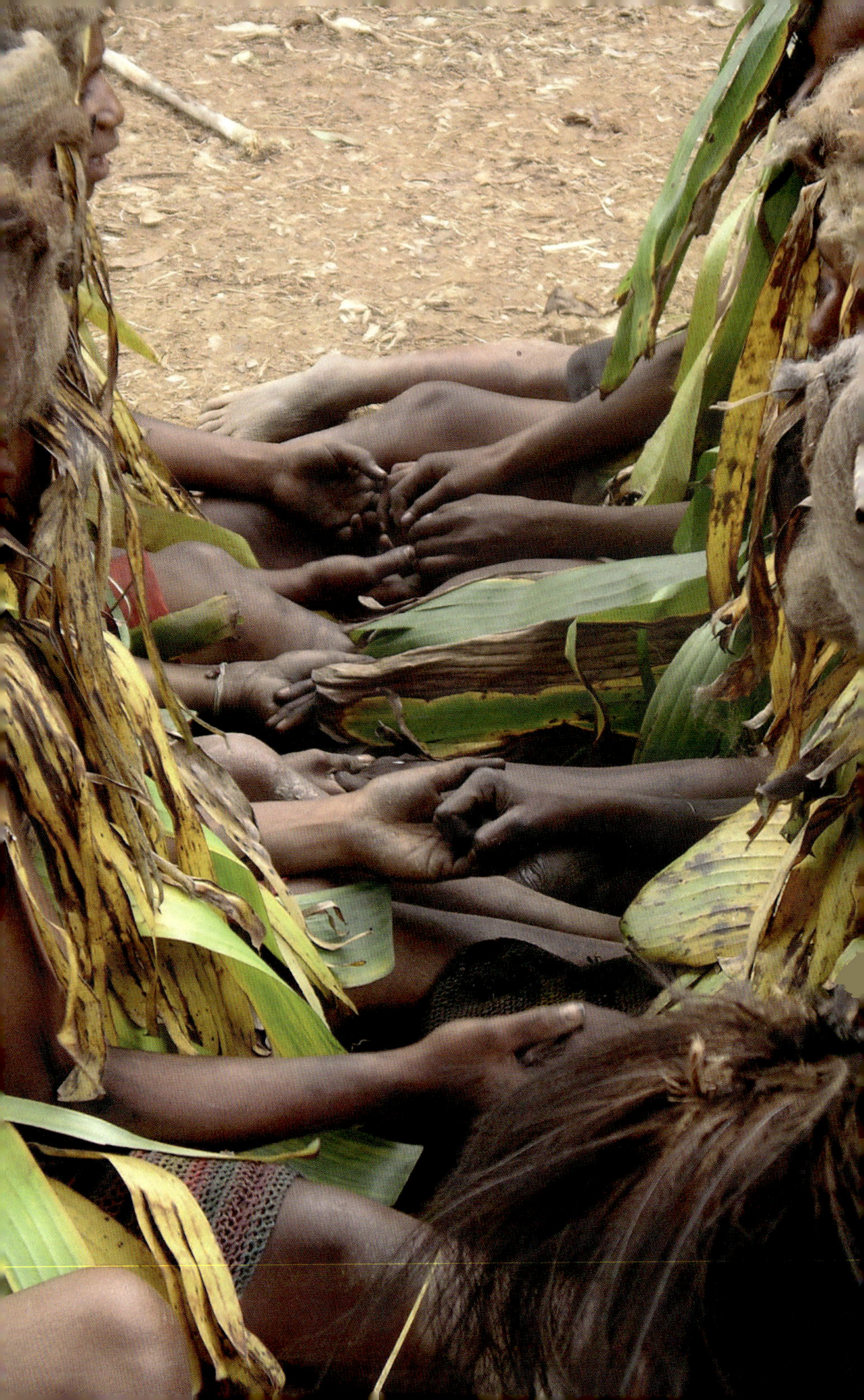

Humans have always been social animals, for good reason: our survival depends on working together because we are not the fastest, strongest or toughest animals on the plains.

Tribes have not forgotten this. Tribal survival is a collective effort. Tribes are teams, but they cannot select their team, nor can they fire low performers.

To meet the team challenge, tribes have evolved effective habits and strong cultures to survive. Not all cultural habits, such as initiation rites, are pleasant. These are covered in the cultural code section.

Tribal teams are role models for modern firms in terms of:

› Good communication
› Effective decision making
› Good use of technology
› Strong culture (separate section)

No individual survives without the team: one for all and all for one.

(left) Communal singing, Papua New Guinea

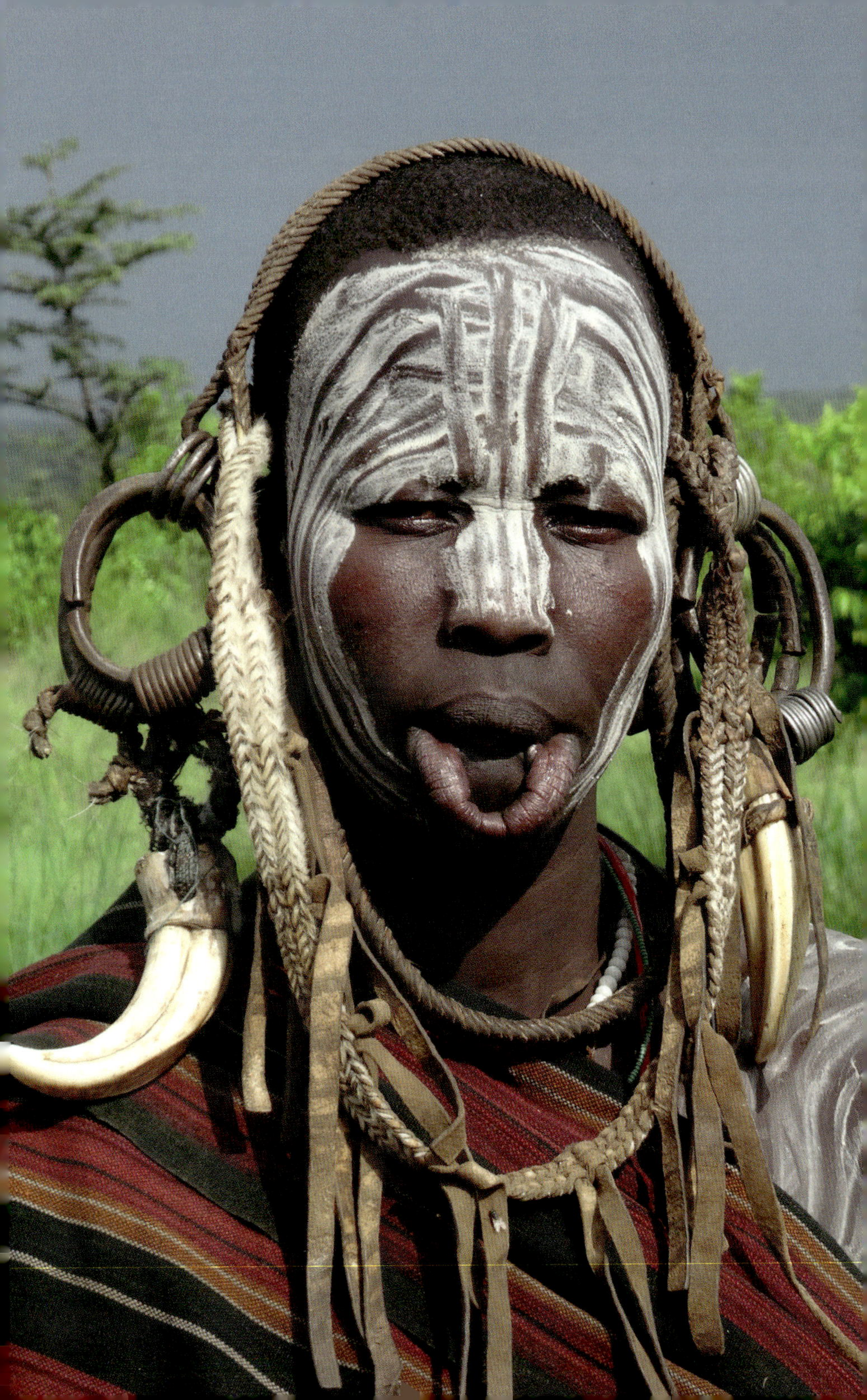

Respect your tribe

All firms are collections of tribes, each with their exotic dress codes and customs. A senior finance professional, a middling sales executive and an IT specialist will all look and act differently. None of these rules are written down anywhere, but you ignore them at your peril. If you want to belong to the tribe, you have to respect your tribe, just as in traditional societies.

The difference between a firm and a tribe is that all tribes are one tribe tribes. They are united in their fight for survival. Their biggest threats are external: competition and weather. Inside a firm, the biggest threats are in theory competition and the economy. But in practice, every manager knows that the real competition is sitting at a hot desk nearby. External competition may steal market share and the bonus for the CEO; internal competition will steal that limited pot of budget, promotions and management time and support for your agenda. In practice, the way firms allocate resources and choose priorities comes from internal competition between ideas and agendas.

Firms struggle to create the one firm firm; tribal instincts are strong. Most firms are a collection of tribes distinguished by function, seniority, geography and line of business. A tribe which fights itself will not survive long.

(left) Mursi, Omo Valley. What are your tribe's customs and dress codes?

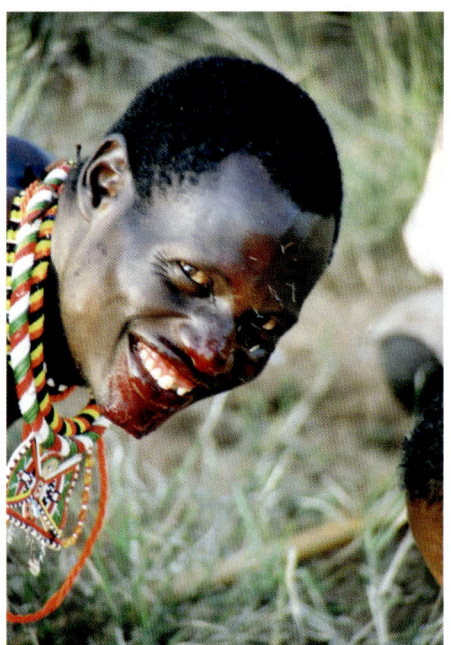

(above) Laikipia preparing the feast. Drinking blood from the throat of a goat as it dies.

(left) it tastes good. Or so I was told…

One for all and all for one: decision making

One morning, Lucy waved her husband goodbye on the way to work. He never came back. He had been murdered in Nairobi. Lucy had no income, no insurance, no job and two kids. So she decided to set up a small clothing business with a tribe she had met.

Chief Kool summoned the village to discuss the idea. The debate raged for two days. How would a white woman cope; what would they do if the business succeeded, or failed? Eventually, they decided to go ahead. Immediately, some villagers found a plot of land for her and started erecting a hut for her. From decision to implementation was immediate.

To celebrate, they killed a goat: they decided together, they implemented together and they feasted together.

The decision worked because it was a fair decision: everyone bought into it. They understood what the decision was, why it mattered and who should do what about it. Like the Japanese, they were slow to build consensus but then fast to act, and there was no going back on the decision.

Decision making should unite and focus your team. Be decisive, not divisive.

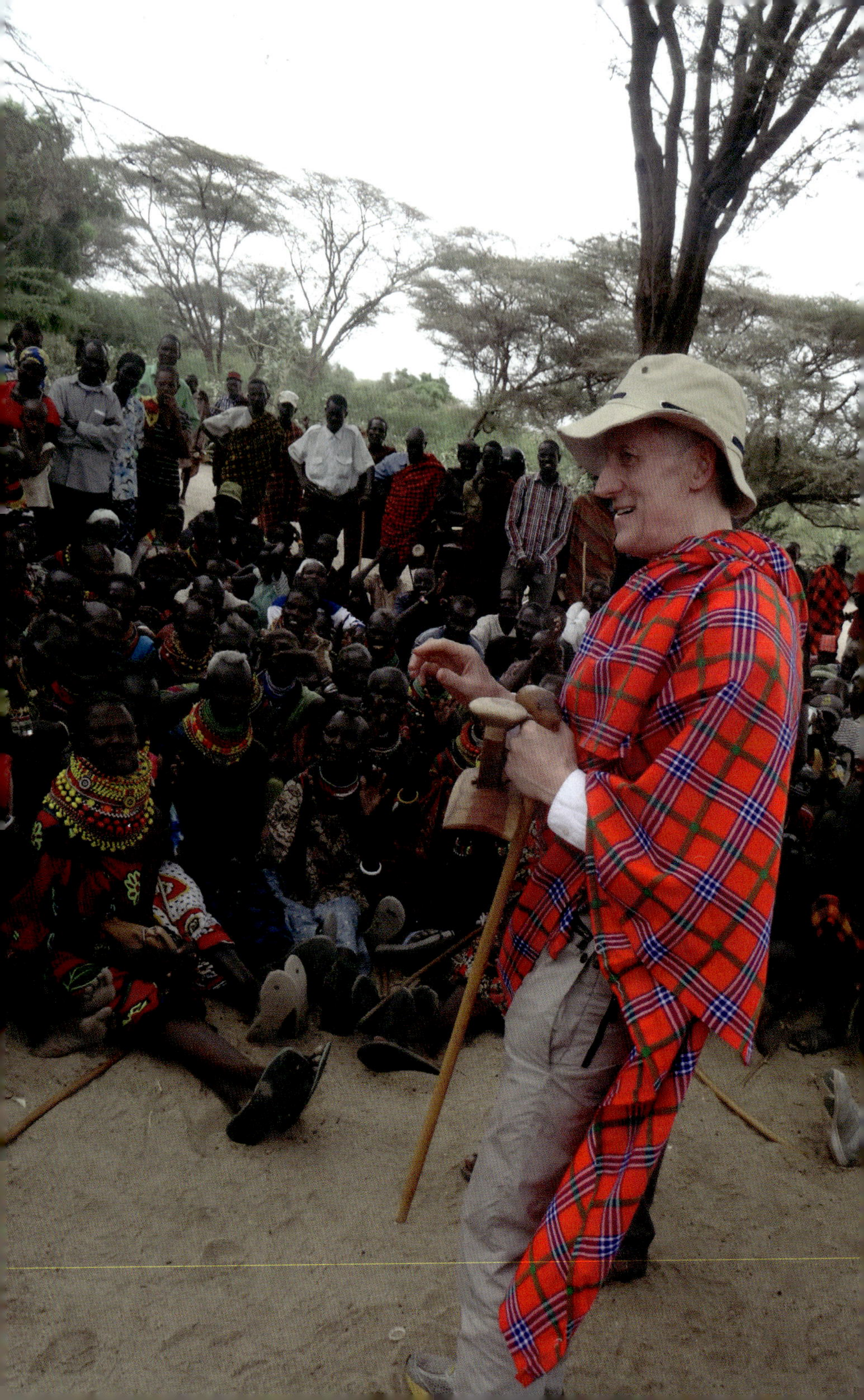

One for all and all for one

Lokichar is a barren place in the middle of an arid zone, near the lawless Somali border. Raiding parties, drought and population pressure are just some of the challenges the local Turkana face.

We went to discuss girls' education: should there be any?

It was a finely balanced debate: educated girls would raise the next generation who could then escape poverty. But an educated girl is worth a smaller dowry (because she might leave, and the longer she stays in education, the less valuable she becomes). And there were practical problems. Girls need latrines, and underwear, and (ideally) a school room.

The village needed to be convinced. So all four hundred villagers got together and talked. And talked. And talked. And then talked some more.

Finally, they decided. The girls would be educated; we would install some latrines. I became an elder of Lokichar.

If you want commitment, do not impose a decision. Use the decision process to ensure collective commitment, effort and success.

(left) The author holding a community conversation in Lokichar, Turkana territory: should the community support girls' education?

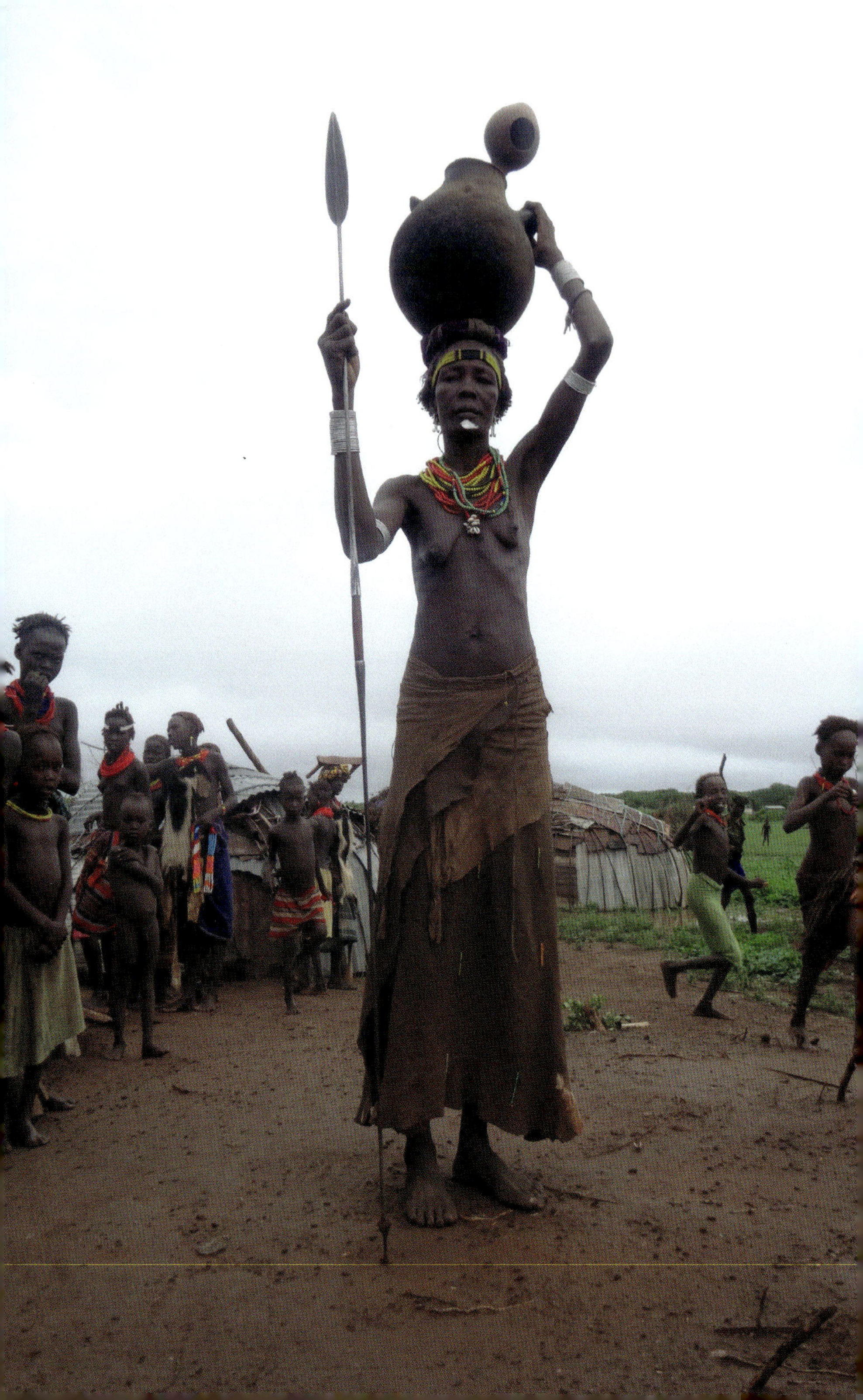

Survival is a collective effort

The Hamar are a very tough tribe. But even they fear the Dassenach. We crossed the river into Dassenach territory and approached the village huts with some trepidation. We were greeted by a fearsome horde of... women and children. The men were expected back in a few months' time from their herding (and raiding) duties.

Every tribe does the same: the old and the young, male and female all have different roles. Everyone contributes whatever they can, even young children. This means that everyone depends on everyone else; that drives real peer group pressure to conform and perform.

Mutual dependence comes not just from specialisation of roles. It also comes from collective tasks such as defence or managing water supplies, which no one can do alone.

Teams in firms often do not know why they have to be a team. Team building workshops are pointless unless you know the point of being a team.

Discover where and when you have mutual dependence, and you discover where and when you need to be a team.

(left) Dassenach village. Lower Omo Valley. Populated only by women and children.

THE TRIBAL CODE

Ancient rock drawings in South West Libya: humanity has always used the latest technology to communicate. An early hunting manual?

Some communication lasts longer than others.

Communicate less, understand more

We communicate more than ever but we understand each other as little as ever.

Tribes do not enjoy the wonders of email and social media. Instead of using social media, they have to be social: they talk to each other. They all gossip: the women gossip, the elders gossip, the warriors gossip and the young play together. They all gossip about different things, but the effect is the same: they all know each other intimately and understand each other closely.

Face to face communication builds understanding and trust. Any misunderstandings are quickly noted and resolved. Technology is wonderful for transactions, but useless for building trust or dealing with human emotions. The first person to work out how to motivate by email will make a fortune: it is a fortune which is unlikely to be made.

Using technology to communicate works where you already have built understanding and trust; otherwise it leads to misunderstanding which festers. This matters in a global world: technology enables global communication, but does nothing to enhance global understanding.

Buy that plane or train ticket: meet your virtual colleagues and build the trust which makes communication work.

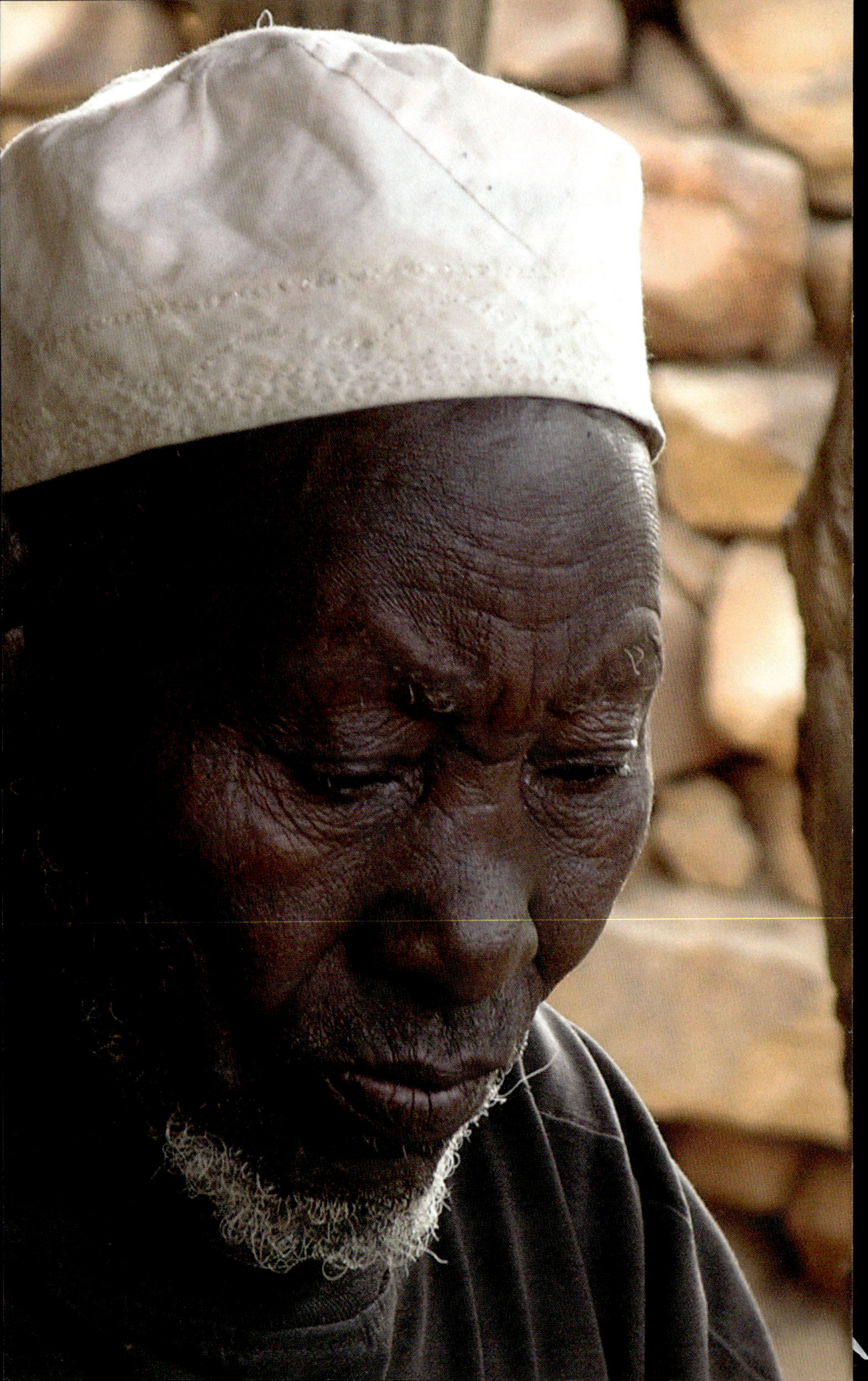

Communicate less: choose your words

I asked the Bambara elder one too many questions. He paused his handiwork and stared intently at me.

"Let me explain" he said patiently. "Words are like gods. Words can create whole new worlds in people's minds. Words can make people do things. With words alone one man can rule so many others. So in our society we respect words.

"A good speaker will forge each idea with the care of a blacksmith, weave each sentence with the skill of a weaver and polish each word brightly, like a silver smith."

With that, he fell silent and the interview was over.

We have gone from an age of too little information to an age of information overload. It is easy to present too long and write too much. Brevity is hard to achieve: it requires strong focus and clear thinking.

Say less, say it better. Make each word count.

(left) Bambara elder at his foot powered loom, Mali

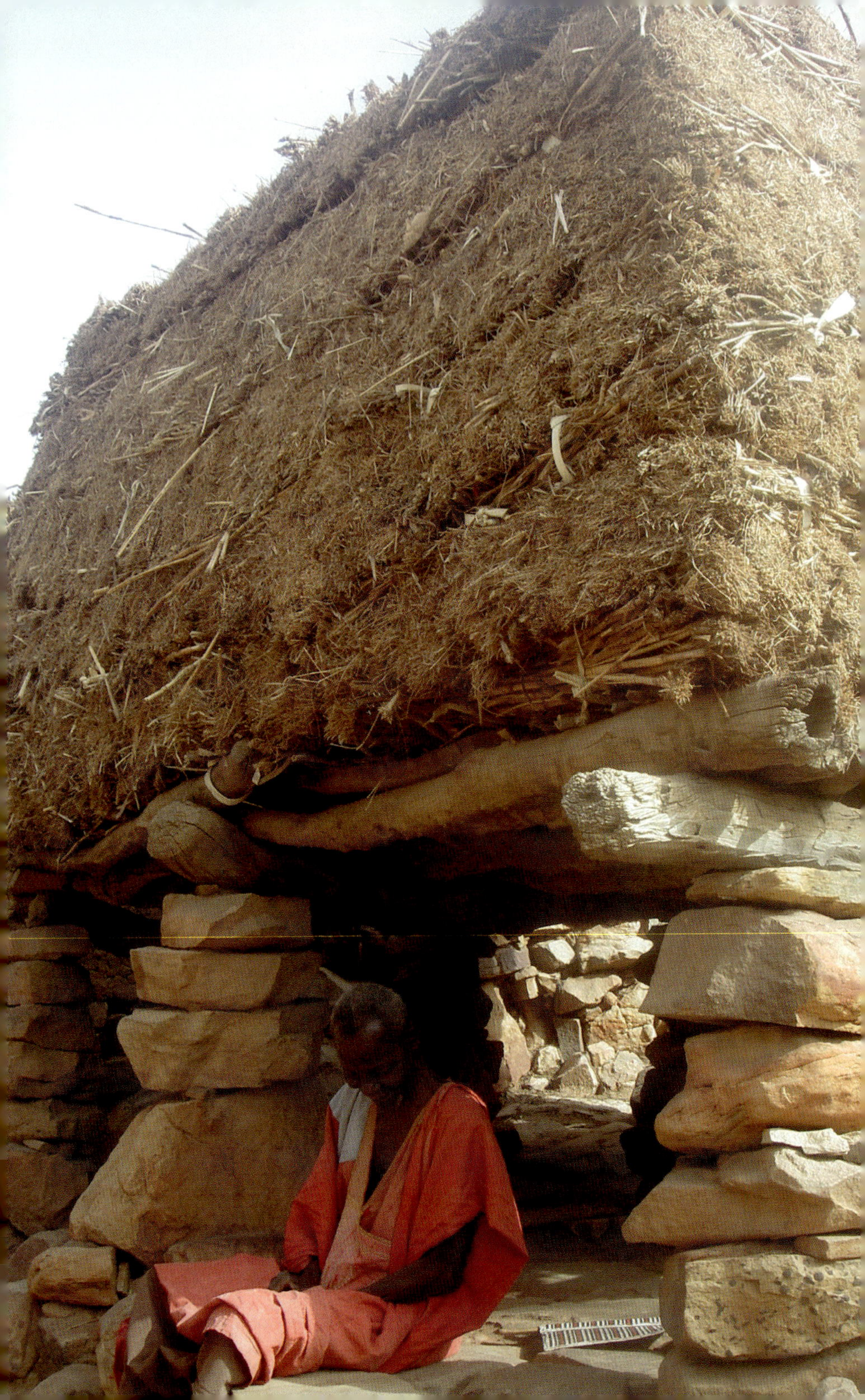

Trust the messenger, not the message

The Dogon elders were gossiping outside the Togana, or village parliament. Each Togana is built with very low ceilings, so that when arguments erupt no one can stand up and hit someone.

The gossip was the normal gossip of village life: local scandals and disputes, the state of the crop and putting the world (and the village) to rights. The gossip was the village information exchange and everyone knew how to process the information. One elder was given to wild exaggeration and theatricals: his forecasts of doom were gently mocked. Another would say little, but to great effect.

The elders were acting like classic venture capitalists: they trusted the messenger, not the message. Everyone knows how to shape a proposal or PowerPoint presentation: they have the credibility of Pravda in the Soviet era. Leaders look beyond the message: a B grade plan from an A* executive is worth far more than A* promises from a B grade executive: you can improve the proposal far more easily than you can improve the executive.

The credibility of your message depends on the credibility of you and your backers.

(left) Dogon elder by the village Parliament or Togana. Note the low ceiling which stops fights breaking out.

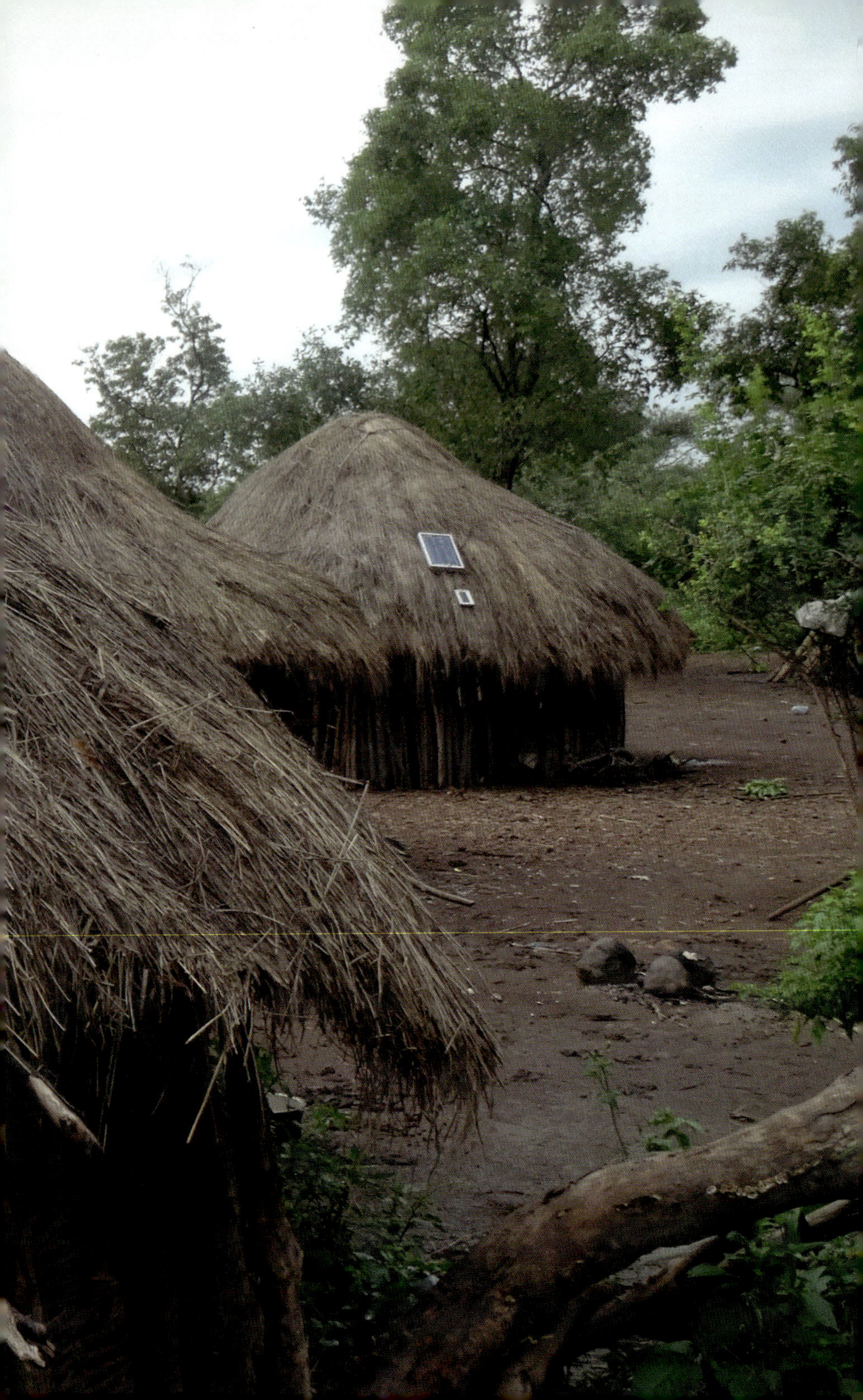

Make technology your servant, not your master

The village had a problem. Its only source of cash was a small coffee crop. They could go to two markets, each a one day round trip walk away, through hostile territory.

Each market was dominated by one coffee factory and buyer, which knew the tribal people would not want to return home with their coffee unsold. So they faced a market rip-off: accept low prices or go home.

Eventually, the tribe found a solution. They bought a second hand mobile phone with a small solar panel to recharge it. Before setting off to market, they check the world price of coffee on the London market, and then call the buyers in both local markets to see who will offer them the best price. They have doubled their income.

Globalisation and technology are transforming even the remotest communities. The tribe has made technology their servant, not their master.

Technology shackles us to the always-on 24/7 treadmill and raises expectations of what we should do: anytime emails, elaborate PowerPoint and becoming our own customer service agents online and at shops.

Technology can free you or enslave you. Make sure you are its master, not its servant.

(left) Mursi Village. Omo Valley. Including the traditional solar panel on the roof of the chief's hut, for his mobile phone.

THE TRIBAL CODE

It helps to work together. Bambara women drawing water together.

The Team Code checklist

1. Survival is a collective effort.
2. Live the values of your team. So join a team which has your values.
3. Effective teams dare to disagree, but not to fight.
4. Don't decide for the team; decide with the team. Build commitment with your decision making process.
5. Good communications requires good trust, which is built face to face. Meet and talk in person, not by email.
6. Good communication does not mean talking louder or longer. Listen more, say less.
7. Where you have mutual dependence you have a team; otherwise you have individual responsibility.
8. High performance requires high commitment: no hiding places.
9. Become the master, not the slave, of technology. 24/7 working is possible, but is it good?
10. Celebrate to survive. Build bonds in the good times to take you through the hard times.

3
THE CHANGE CODE

Change or die

Migrate to greener pastures

Control your destiny, or someone else will

Shillingi's life map, which indicated he was over 120 years old. Tribal stories make a point better than they recount history. Life revolves around the village (centre). Laikipia, northern Kenya.

His life story starts top left, works clockwise through a bloodbath until he starts looking after the animals he has been killing (middle left).

Change or die

Shillingi got his name because he took the King's shilling (and boots and army uniform) and then promptly disappeared into the bush with his swag.

He recounted his life story. It was a heroic blood bath of killing lions, elephants and other beasts. And then in the very final scene, he is looking after all the animals he used to kill. What happened?

Shillingi explained: "we had a drought for four years. All the animals were dying. If they die, we die. So now we look after the animals. Instead of killing animals, we want to farm tourists!"

As corporate transformation programmes go, that is as radical as they come: from killing animals to farming tourists. But it is better than the opposite: from farming animals to killing tourists.

Shillingi had discovered an essential truth: if you want to survive, you have to change.

THE TRIBAL CODE

Mongolian Steppe where nothing changes except the seasons (top)…
until you look closer (bottom).

Change because you want to...

At first sight, nothing seems to change for the nomads of Mongolia, other than the seasons of the year.

But look closer and it is clear that they want to change: the lure of satellite television and phones extends deep into the Steppe.

Most traditional societies want to change: we may think that they are picturesque, but poverty, disease and hard work is not picturesque to them. They do not want to be our photo opportunity.

The Dogon elder was blunt: "we see visitors from town. They are stupid: they do not know how to build a house or farm a crop. But they are rich: they have phones and televisions. How is this? Why should I not want this for my children?"

Traditional societies value their traditions, but they value progress even more. Sometimes, you have to let go of the past to reach the future.

THE TRIBAL CODE

Saami reindeer deal with the Arctic winter (top) better than they deal with fences and national borders (bottom).

...change because you must

The Saami have been herding reindeer down from the mountains to the sea every spring since time immemorial. But even the reindeer and their herders have to keep up with the times.

However good the reindeer are at surviving an Arctic winter, they are rubbish at property law. Fences really confuse them: they can migrate through ice, but not through fences.

This fence is also a national border. To the north is Norway where the Saami and the reindeer still migrate. To the south, Finland where the Saami are settled into farms. That means no migration: the Finnish Saami have switched from herding reindeer to farming EU reindeer subsidies.

While the Finnish Saami had to change, the Norwegian Saami wanted to change. Herding reindeer is hard work: in 36 hours you might snatch 30 minutes of sleep on the back of a snowmobile. But that is luxury compared to the past: snowmobiles beat snow shoes every day.

Sometimes you have to change, sometimes you want to change. Either way, you change.

THE TRIBAL CODE

Find your pasture: horses in the green ocean of the Mongolian Steppe (above) and 700 reindeer in the frozen white ice desert of the Arctic (below)

Migrate to greener pastures

Nomads by their nature are on the move regularly, in search of survival. They have an advantage over modern firms: they know where the green pastures will be, when to go there and what (if any) competition exists.

Modern firms can not be sure if they are heading towards the green pastures or the frozen white ice desert; nor do they know what competition will be there.

While nomads keep moving in a predictable cycle, firms have to keep moving forward. Since the future is inherently unknowable, firms which are the most adaptable, which test and change most effectively are the ones which will survive. Find your green pastures, look for uncompeted spaces and protect what you have.

But both nomads and firms know that staying still is fatal. The future may be uncertain, but failure to migrate is certain failure.

THE TRIBAL CODE

Uncle Jack, founder of a successful Aborigine community near Kununurra. Western Australia/Northern Territory border.

Control your destiny, or someone else will

Uncle Jack was rightly proud of the community he had set up in the Outback near Kununurra. But he had no time for his Aboriginal cousins in town: "They have nothing to look forward to, except dice, drugs, drink, dole and death".

It was not meant to be that way. After World War II, the government tried to help by integrating the Aborigines into European society: the boys became stockmen, and the girls went into domestic service. The result was unpaid abuse. So the government insisted they should be paid properly. As a result, they all lost their jobs and went on the dole. They had lost their original culture and not gained a new one.

Similar stories can be told of the Saami in Norway and the Inuit in Canada. The road to hell is paved with good (government) intentions.

Change is always hazardous. Destroying things is easy, creating a new way is hard.

If change is done to you, you will be a victim of change. If you lead the change, you have a chance of success. Control your destiny, or someone else will.

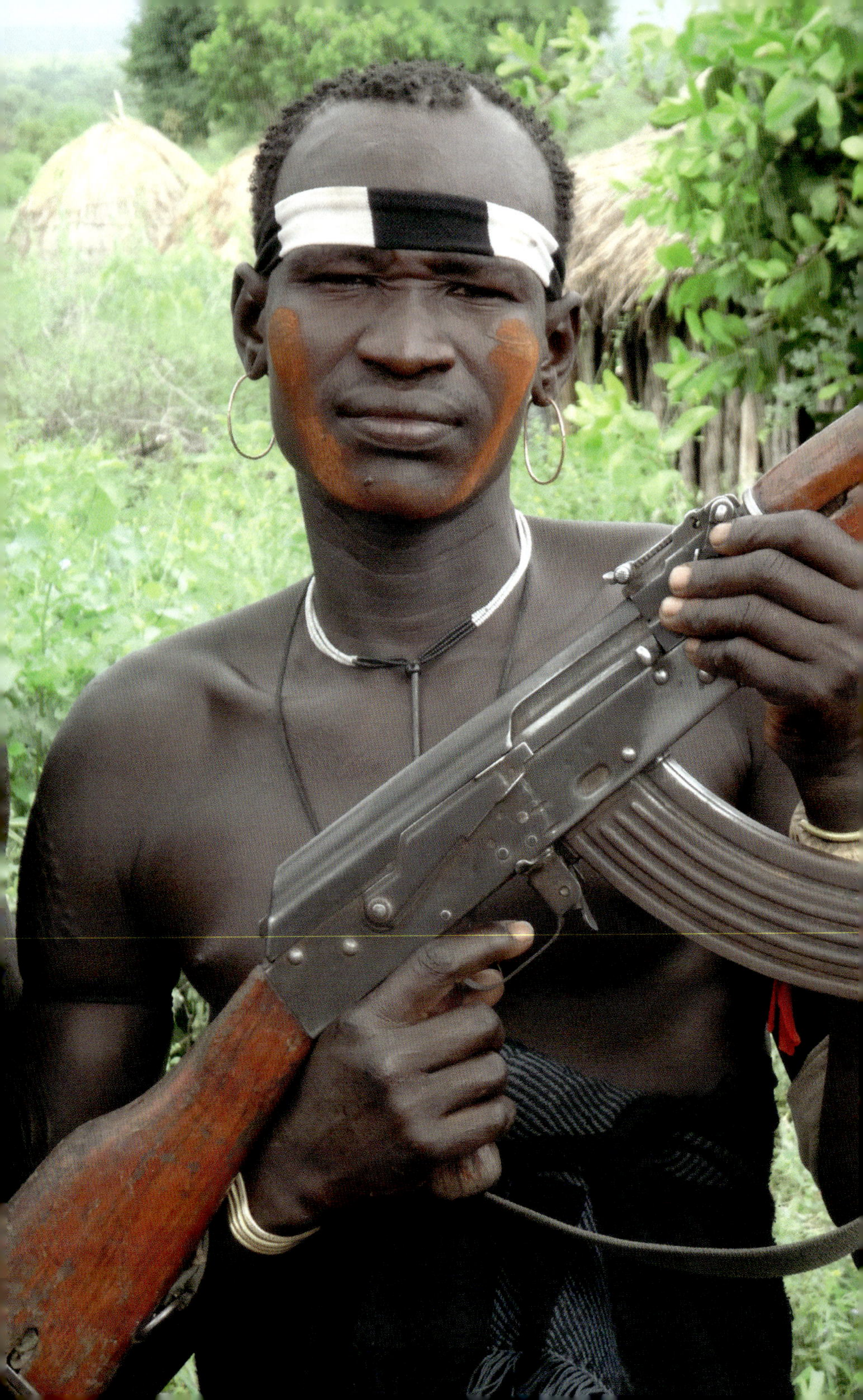

All change

All tribes are tribes in transition: some because they want to, some because they have to. This is the inevitable: if tribal survival is about fit, not perfection, then tribes have to change as the world changes. Yesterday's formula for survival will not work tomorrow, if tomorrow is different. The ideas of "fit" and "change" are two sides of the same coin.

The pressure for change is everywhere you look:

- Increased competition: the arrival of guns
- Pressure from commercial farms and land grabs
- Population pressure and resource competition
- Climate change and resource pressure
- Desire for material advancement

Failure to change means failure to survive. If the tribe goes out of business, they have no welfare to fall back on and they cannot sign up for interviews to join another tribe.

Change or die.

(left) Guns increase the pressure for change.

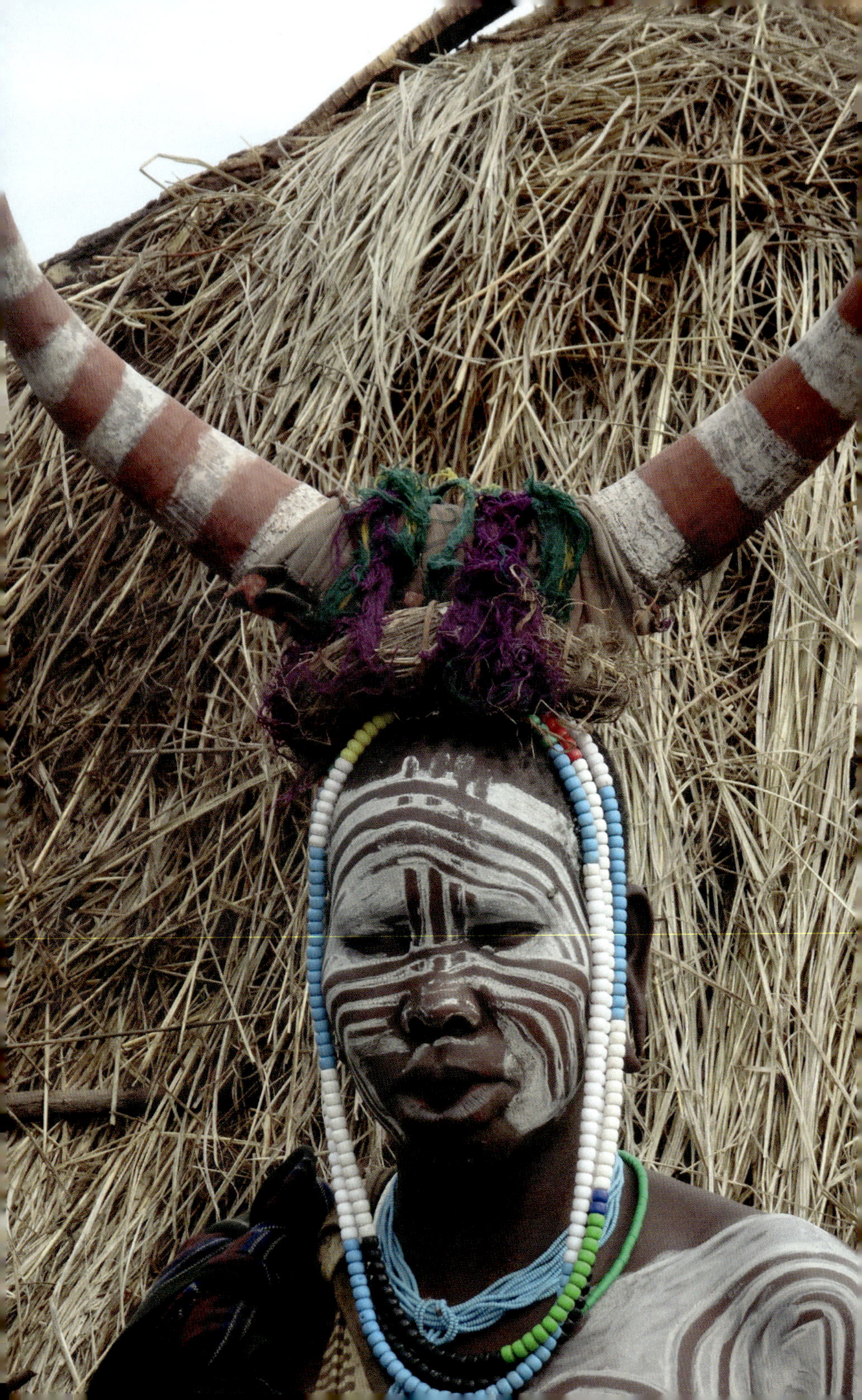

The Change Code checklist

1. The world is changing and will not stop for you, or for anyone else.
2. Survival means you have to change.
3. Success means you keep on changing.
4. Be prepared to let go of your past: what worked before may not work in future.
5. All change is hazardous, especially when it is done to you and not by you.
6. Control your destiny, or someone else will: embrace change, don't fight it.
7. You can hope to get lucky, but hope is not a method and luck is not a strategy. Take control of your future.
8. Know what you want, otherwise you are unlikely to get what you want.
9. When your context changes, the rules of survival and success change.
10. Change because you have to, change because you want to. Either way, change.

(left) Mursi female. Even the most traditional tribes want to change or have to change.

4
THE STRATEGY CODE

Seek fit, not perfection

Focus, focus, focus

Unfair fights are the best fights

Defend what you have

Escape the resource trap

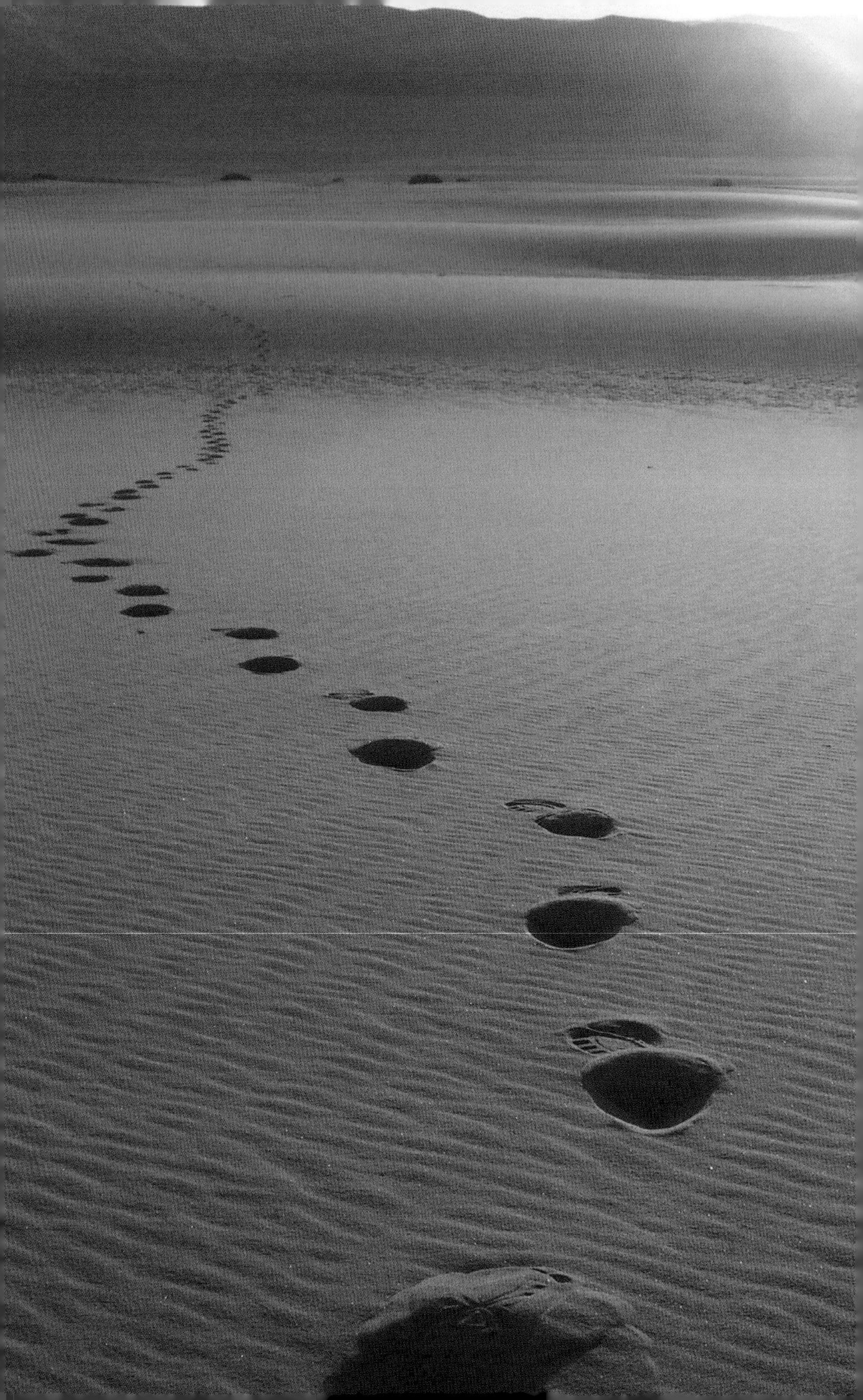

Journeys of discovery

Most tribes cannot afford to hire McKinsey to design their future. Instead, they take responsibility for their own future. Lacking all the formal strategy tools of business schools they do something better than designing their future: they discover their future.

Tribal strategy is the product of endless trial and error. Bad strategies are a welcome sign to the four horsemen of the apocalypse: death, war, famine and conquest. Because the stakes are so high, each tribe has discovered the survival strategy which works for them in their context.

Tribal strategies vary widely, but have the same basic principles:

Discover, don't design your future: do they realise that they use strategic intent and core competencies as their approach to strategy?

Seek fit, not perfection. And when the context changes, the tribe changes: change is constant

Focus, focus, focus. Confusion and internal conflict are luxuries which firms, but not tribes, can afford.

Unfair fights are the best fights. When survival is on the line, you cannot afford to lose.

Sahara, SW Libya. All strategy is a journey of discovery.

The Perfect Predator, designed by committee. Painting: Haydn Cornner
The committee of gurus went on to design the perfect leader…

Seek fit, not perfection: the excellence myth

Try this exercise: design the perfect predator.

We decided to do this. Each of us took responsibility for one limb. The result was a beast with the ears of an elephant, jaws of a crocodile, neck of a giraffe, hide of a rhino, the legs of a cheetah and the tail of a scorpion. The poor beast promptly died of its own improbability, but not before we managed to get a picture of it.

Now try to design the perfect leader.

If you read leadership books, you will find that leaders are empowering and directing; bold and humble; visionary and detailed; analytical with a bias to action; focused on the long term and short term; supportive and ruthless. They are a cornucopia of contradictions. Like the perfect predator, they expire on first contact with reality, because no leader gets ticks in all the boxes.

Finally, try to design the perfect firm.

Countless gurus claim to have the essence of excellence or greatness. Like the quack doctors of the Wild West, they claim to cure everything from limping competitiveness to a drooping share price. They invite you to buy the book, surf the fad, hear the presentation, take the pill and then… nothing happens.

Searching for perfection is like searching for smoke signals in the fog: it is an exercise in futility.

THE TRIBAL CODE

(above) Reindeer in the Arctic.
(below) Lion tracking the wildebeest migration, Tanzania.

Which is the better survivor? What happens if they swap contexts?

Seek fit, not perfection: reindeers or lions?

The thermometer could record all the way down to -20° centigrade. It was useless. It was not registering anything: it was too cold. We had been up for 36 hours non-stop as we followed the reindeer on their annual migration from the mountains to the sea. It was a miracle that they could survive in the frozen white ice desert of the Arctic, pausing to eat bits of lichen on rocks protruding through the ice.

Had the reindeer discovered the essence of survival?

Months later and thousands of miles away we watched a pride of lions following the wildebeest on their annual migration. The lions are top predators, and the wildebeest try to steer well clear of them.

So are lions the true kings of the jungle (or plains)?

To choose between the lions and reindeer, try switching them around.

> A lion in the Arctic would not be a happy lion.

> A reindeer in the Serengeti is called "lunch."

There is no universal idea of excellence: there is only what works in your context today. And because your context is always changing, you always have to change.

Don't seek a universal formula for excellence. Work out what works in your context, and then change as your context changes. Focus on fit, not excellence.

THE TRIBAL CODE

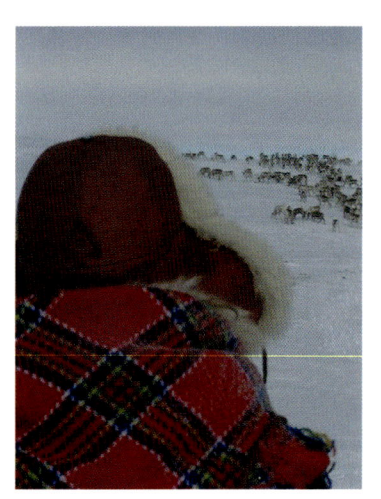

(clockwise from top left) Laikipia girls, Bari in Papua New Guinea, Saami herding reindeer, Tuareg in SW Libya.

The tribal fitness programme

The diversity of traditional societies is astonishing, and not just for what they wear (see opposite).

There are pastoralists, hunter gatherers, settled farmers, traders, and fishing communities. They may organise by family, village or region. They exist in the frozen wastes of the Arctic, through the green grass ocean of the Steppe to the golden sands of the Sahara, into jungles and beyond.

No tribe claims to have a universal solution to tribal survival and success. Like the lion and the reindeer, if you swap their environments around, they would struggle. Instead, each tribe has adapted perfectly to their context.

Business theory is the land of fad and fashion; each new fad promises a universal solution to success. Tribes show that this is nonsense. There is no universal solution to strategy or success. There is only what works for you in your context.

Survival is about fitness: how well you fit your context. If you learn and adapt fast, you will survive.

THE TRIBAL CODE

The Great Wall snaking along the border of climates and civilisations. Different strategies and types of organisation exist each side of the Wall.

Fit your context

For tribes, geography is everything. Each traditional society adapts itself to its context.

Travelling from the Mongolian Steppe towards China is to experience the shock of seeing fences for the first time: that means the advent of private property.

The biggest fence of all is the Great Wall, built along the line of roughly 20cm rainfall a year. North and west of the Wall is too dry for farming: the nomads reign supreme.

The difference was caught by a friendship treaty of 198BC which says: "let the state holding the bows beyond the Great Wall follow the rules of the Shanui, and let the Han govern the state of the overcoat and hat which lie inside the Great Wall."

The two sides were divided by rainfall, a wall and different modes of survival. Neither system was perfect, but they worked in context.

Don't search for perfection. Search for fit

THE TRIBAL CODE

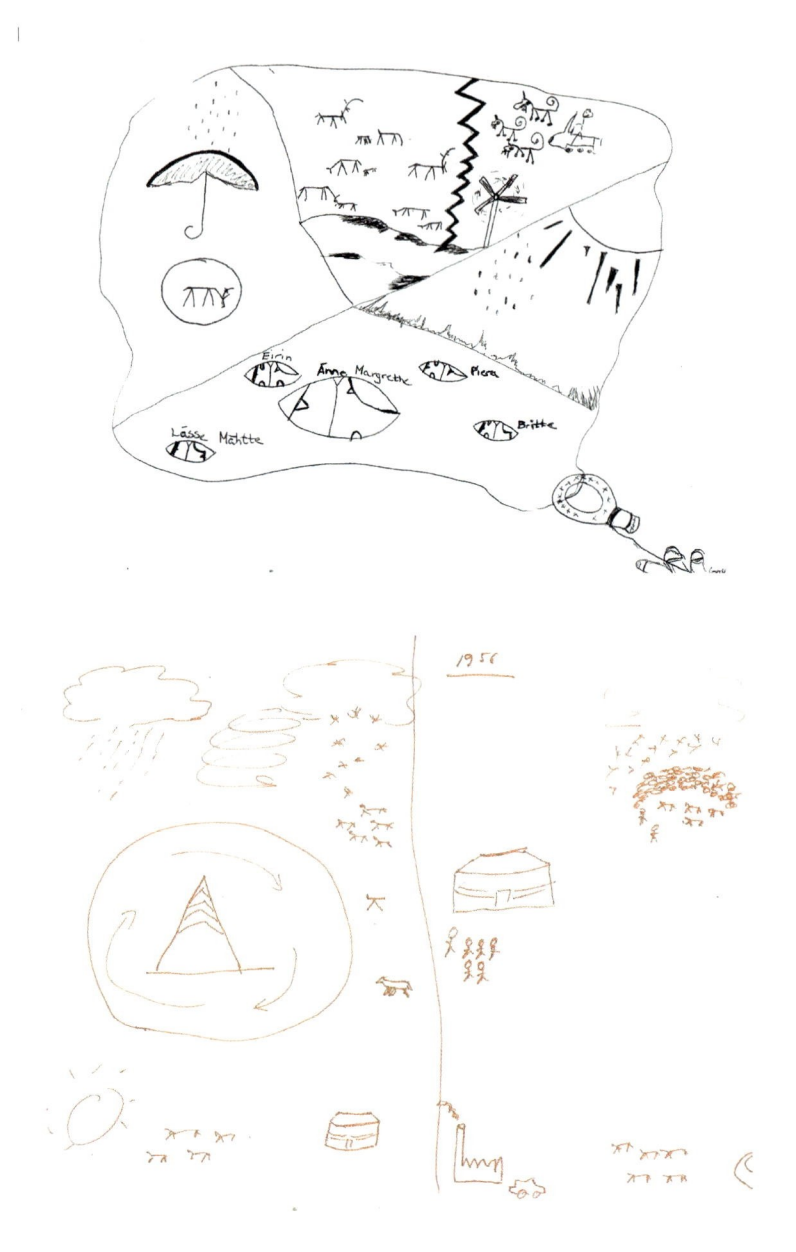

The Saami map (above) and Mongolian nomad map (below) offer the same solutions to the same challenges.

Fit your context

I asked the Saami to draw their territory. They drew their territory as a year, (opposite, above) with four distinct seasons. This includes a harsh winter and a deadly spring. In winter, reindeer can kick through snow to find grazing. A cold snap in spring creates a layer of ice which they cannot penetrate to get to their grazing

As nomads, traditionally it made sense for them to follow their herds. It also means they take a dim view of encroachment on their traditional lands by people trying to buy property or by governments trying to build wind farms.

Thousands of miles away, the nomads in Mongolia face the same challenges: poor soil and four distinct seasons including harsh winters and a deadly spring.

The Saami and Mongolian nomads have the same responses to the same challenges: they organise themselves along family lines and are nomadic: they follow their herds over the year. That in turn gives rise to notions of shared land rights, not private property rights.

You can not know your strategy and you cannot build your organisation until you really understand your context.

THE TRIBAL CODE

The Tuareg caravan map (above): all that matters is water. Make sure your oasis has sweet, not salt, water (below).

Focus, focus, focus

The Tuareg were leading the salt caravan across the Sahara to Timbuktu. I asked them to draw a map of their territory and what was important in it.

The result looked disappointing. I asked them about the scene at the top. The Tuareg replied: "you ask what is important? That is a well. For water. That is what is important in the desert."

I asked about the scene at the bottom. Patiently, the Tuareg explained. "That is also a well. For water. So now you know what matters most to us in the desert."

Finally, I asked about what looked like small animals with their legs in the air, near the top well. Exasperated, the Tuareg said: "they are water bags. For water. In the desert, that is all that matters."

What is the most important thing for yourself and your firm: what must you protect at all costs?

THE TRIBAL CODE

Wrestling at Choidog's nadaam (festival) in Mongolia. The problem with a fair fight is that you might lose it.

Unfair fights are the best fights

CEOs claim to like competition. To expose this lie, ask them if they like losing. The problem with a fair fight is that you might lose it. CEOs do not like competing: they like winning.

The best firms are like the best tribes: they have a source of thoroughly unfair competitive advantage. Warren Buffett preferred to invest in firms "which any fool can run, because some day some fool will run it." Unfair advantage makes any firm idiot proof.

Some sources of unfair advantage include:

- A near monopoly on desk top operating systems
- Ownership of the lowest cost oil fields
- Landing rights at Heathrow airport
- Network effects for the top social media and search firms
- Copyright for an image library or music backlist
- Brand ownership
- Patent on a vital medicine

What is your source of unfair advantage?

THE TRIBAL CODE

Hadza cold pressed arrow (above) using the sap of the desert rose shrub for poison, and Hadza hunter (below)

Unfair fights are the best fights: how to kill a lion

To come of age, each cohort of young Laikipia warriors are meant to kill a lion. So how do you kill a lion when you have no guns?

A brave warrior might take the lion on in unarmed combat. The lion would win.

Instead, the Laikipia wait until they stumble across a sleeping lion upwind of them, so they can approach unseen and unsmelled. They put some poison on an arrow, shoot the lion and run like crazy: there is likely to be an annoyed lion nearby.

Over the next 24 hours the poison takes effect and the lion dies. The warriors cut its tail off and go back the village in triumph and trepidation: gruesome initiation rites await them.

None of this is fair on the poor lion. It is not meant to be fair: it is meant to be effective.

THE TRIBAL CODE

Hadza hunter pulling wings of chick (above) to make it call its mother, which they then capture (below) and eat.

Unfair fights are the best fights: hunting birds

How do you hunt birds, without nets, guns or wings? This is the challenge the Hadza face. They are hunter gatherers: if they catch nothing today, they eat nothing today. The local wildlife have learned to avoid the Hadza.

The Hadza change the rules of the game: they play on their terms. When they see a bird's nest on the ground, they investigate. The parents fly away, but the chicks cannot. The Hadza do not kill the chicks. They take them, and stretch the chicks' wings so that they call for their parents. When the parents return, they are easily killed. Not fair on the birds, but the Hadza get to eat.

Facing more nimble or more powerful competitors, you cannot win on their terms. Find a way to fight on your terms. Asymmetric warfare is the only way to beat strong or nimble competition.

Are you competing on your terms, or on the terms of your competition?

THE TRIBAL CODE

(above) Hamar herder at home. Guns are everywhere.
(below) Would you fight over a camel? Author with friends.
Photo: Anthony Willoughby

Know when to fight

A lost camel wandered into the settlement. A camel represents serious wealth. It seemed like Christmas had come early. What would you do with this gift?

The markings on the camel showed it came from a neighbouring tribe, with whom they had a running feud. Immediately, the elders summoned a boy to take the camel back to where it came from. They did not need a war over a lost camel. The boy returned with two goats: a gift from their neighbours. The feud was over, for the moment.

Tribes intuitively understand Sun Tzu, who wrote *The Art of War* 2,500 years ago. He laid out three preconditions of warfare:

> Only fight when there is a prize worth fighting for

> Only fight when you know you will win

> Only fight when you have no other way of achieving your goal

The lost camel failed all three of Sun Tzu's preconditions. It is often better to win an ally than win a war.

Most corporate battles fail at least one, and often all three, of Sun Tzu's preconditions. Know when to fight, and then fight to win.

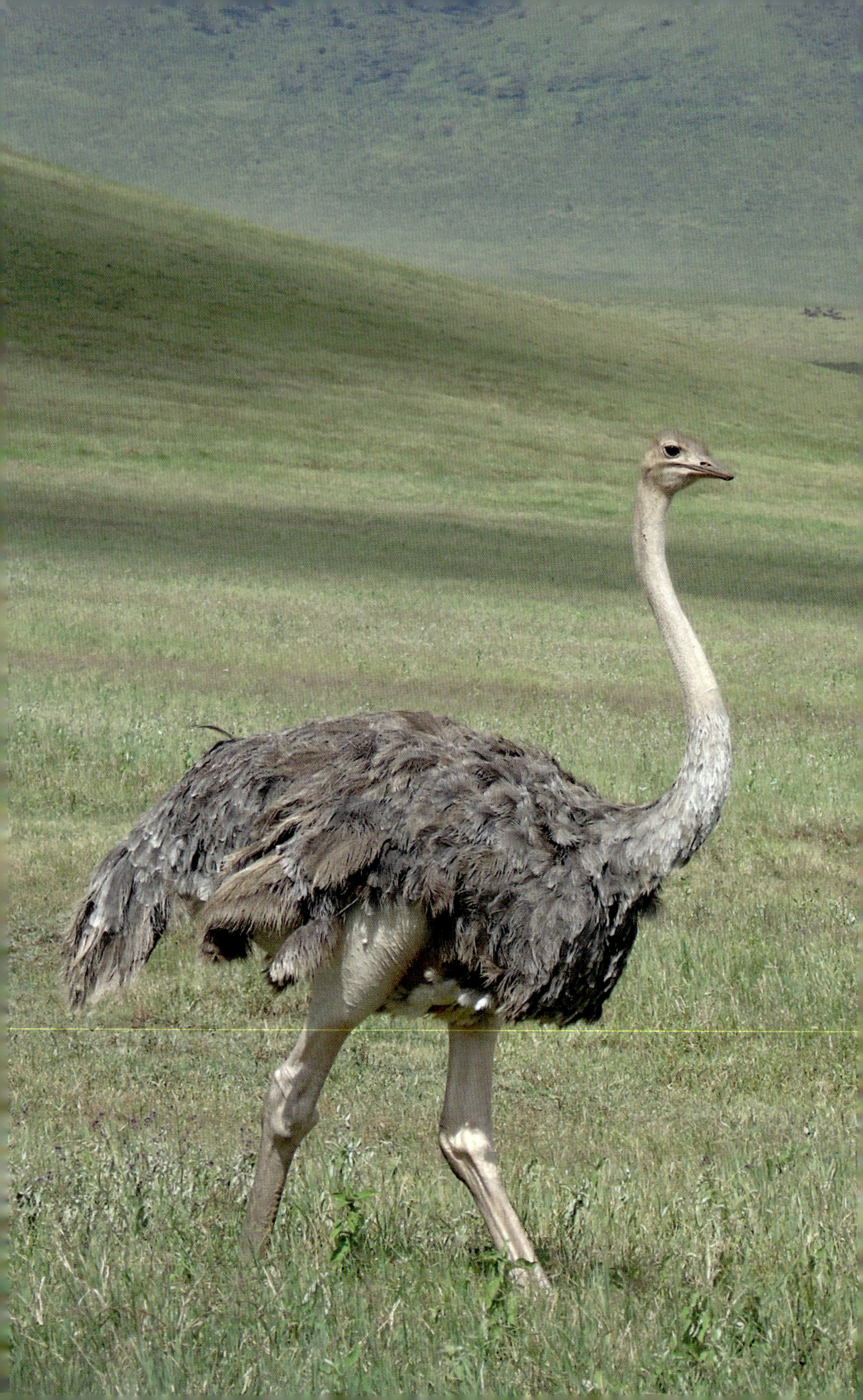

Crises

Never mess with a randy ostrich. I was crossing its territory so it decided to disembowel me. Unfortunately, Ostriches are one of the fastest land animals on earth. Fortunately, I was faster than my companions. Being killed by a lion is one thing, but being killed by a randy ostrich…I would have died of shame.

We all like to think that crises, fraud, corruption and bad stuff is what happens to other people. Wrong. It will happen to you and your firm, but you do not know when, where or why it will happen. There are some simple rules for dealing with crises:

Get help. Lone heroes land up as dead heroes.

Be flexible. No plan survives first contact with reality.

Be open. You need to hear about problems before they become crises. Avoid a blame culture.

Drive to action. If being attacked by an ostrich do not call for a situation report: run for your life.

Stay positive. You will be remembered for how you were, not just for what you did. There is humour even in an ostrich crisis. If you survive.

(left) Ostrich. Ngorongoro crater. At least this one is not randy and homicidal.

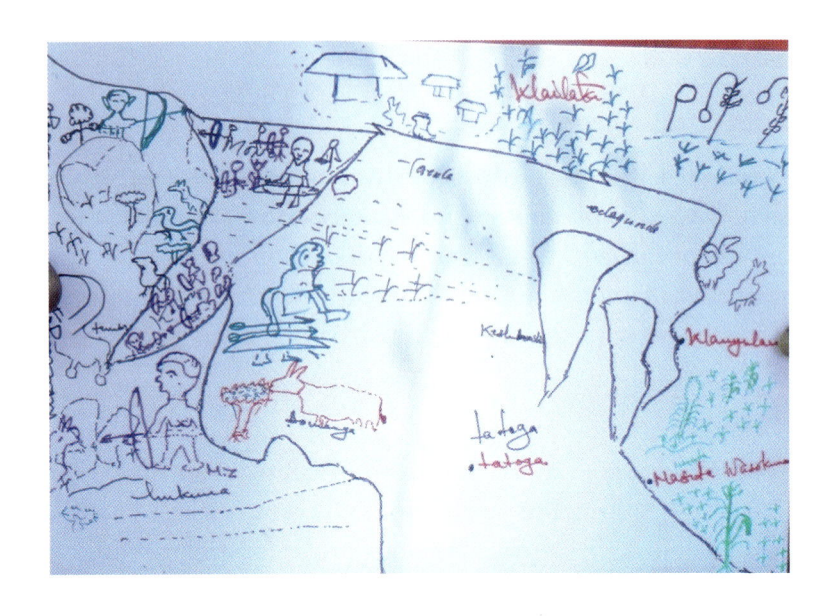

Hadza territory map (above) and Datoga life map (below)

Defend what you have

The Hadza had some trouble drawing their territory map: they had to find someone who knew how to hold a pen. But they certainly know how to hold a spear, and they know exactly where their territory is, even if they cannot draw it well. They defend their territory at all costs.

Hadza are hunter gatherers. Their map shows that they are under threat from agriculture in the north and Datoga pastoralists in the south.

When I visited the Datoga, it was clear where the pressure was coming from. Botolo drew his life map, which was focused around his village. But huge numbers of children in his map, plus droughts, mean that the Datoga have to find more pasture: they have to encroach on Hadza territory.

If you lose your territory, you lose everything. Gurus may urge you to re-engineer a co-created blue ocean new paradigm. That is exciting. But in the meantime, do not lose focus on what pays the rent today.

Growth is only possible if you have a sustainable base. Defend what you have.

THE TRIBAL CODE

Hadza smoking out bees for their honey, and being generously stung for his efforts (above) and learning traditional ways (below)

Embrace risk

When you live on the edge, any minor setback has the potential to be a major disaster. If the Hadza do not succeed in their daily hunt, they go hungry. They have no fall back, no savings, no fridge or freezer they can call on.

Not surprisingly, tribal societies are highly risk averse. They cannot afford failure. Firms also have high ambivalence to risk. No one ever got fired for failing to take a risk. And yet firms want to be innovative and entrepreneurial, without ever failing. If you have never failed, you have not pushed yourself far enough.

In reality, you can only make progress by taking risk: try new ideas, invest in new products, markets, processes and systems. For most firms, risk taking is not a life or death proposition as it is for tribes: firms have more resources to fall back on. Leaders can also take risk, because even if it goes horribly wrong you will not die: you can always move elsewhere.

Avoiding risk is a good survival formula; taking risk is a vital part of your success formula. Risk taking separates survival from success. If you take risk, you accelerate your career: you succeed fast or you fail fast. But if you fail, you can always try again.

Risk management is not about avoiding risk, it is about knowing when and how to take risk.

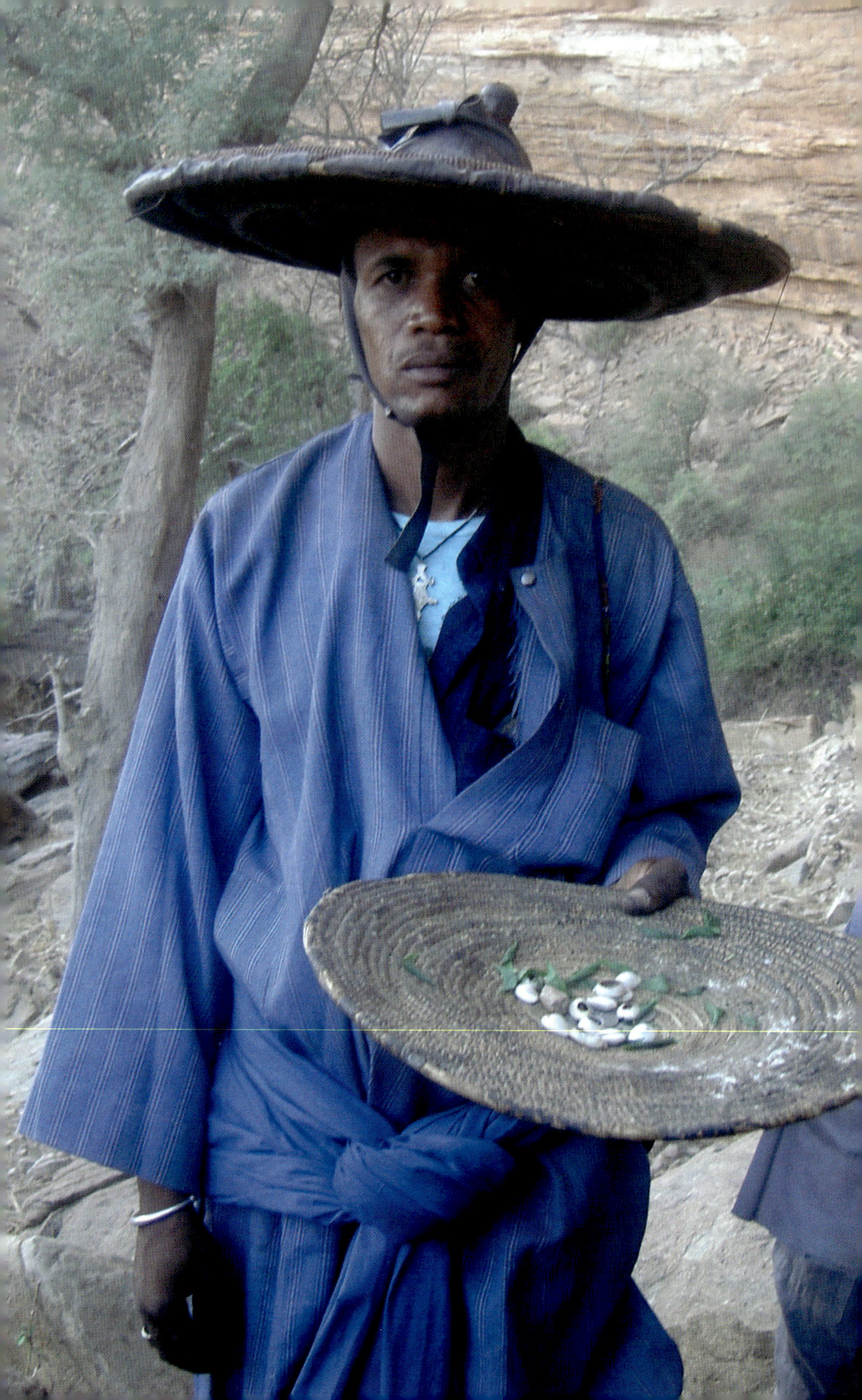

Escape the prison of success

The Dogon fortune teller was very good. He promised me a small fortune in the future, and charged me a great fortune in the present.

But in reality, it is easy to tell the future for tribes and businesses. For most tribes, most of the time, next year will be pretty much the same as last year. For most firms, next year's budget and strategy will be pretty much like last year's, plus or minus a bit.

Tribes and businesses are smart: they do not give up their success formula willingly. But a success formula is like a golden prison from which there is no escape. The prison of success is fine for as long as the world does not change. But when the world changes, the tribe and the firm has to change. The fact that only 27 of the original 100 members of the FTSE 100 still exist shows how hard it is for successful firms to change. When the world changes, the prison of success becomes the prison of failure, and it is hard to escape.

Leaders face the same challenge of the prison of success. What worked for you at one level in one context will not work for you at another level and in another context.

Tribes, businesses and leaders have to keep on adapting to succeed.

(opposite) Dogon fortune teller, Mali

THE TRIBAL CODE

Tribal gaming technology: a chequers board made from cardboard and old bottle tops.

Escape the resource trap

The school was in a barren dust bowl. On the ground, there was a scrap of cardboard and some old bottle tops (see opposite). The children had made a chequers board for themselves. Who needs the latest gaming apps?

Every firm faces the challenge of doing more with less. Tribes show how very little can go very far. It is the same with start-ups which have to make every penny count.

There are two ways to deal with lack of resources. The tribal way is to use less resource. They are world class at lean survival.

The alternative way is to seek more resources: that means borrowing and risk taking. For tribes, taking risks such as planting a new type of crop means you might starve or die if it goes wrong. Tribes are deeply risk averse, which keeps them in the low resource trap.

It is not just firms which escape the resource trap by taking risk and investing. Start-ups and individual teams and functions do the same. Every time you bid for more budget you have to commit to delivering more in return: you make a promise and take a risk.

Tribal survival is about low risk with low resources. Firms have can escape the resource trap with investment and managed risk.

If you never take a risk, you never succeed. Risk is key to success.

THE TRIBAL CODE

Crossing the river out of hostile territory on to home territory, on the way back from market. Seek safety in numbers. Happy group and relieved author. Papua New Guinea. Photo: Anthony Willoughby

The Strategy Code checklist

1. Don't seek perfection: find out what works for you in your context.
2. Because your context keeps changing, you have to keep changing.
3. Unfair fights are the best fights. The problem with a fair fight is that you might lose it.
4. Use asymmetric warfare: fight on your terms, not your opponents'.
5. Focus, focus, focus: know what you must protect at all costs.
6. Fads, fashions and theory are dangerous. Discover what works in practice, not in theory.
7. It is better to win an ally than win a fight: the best victories are gained without a fight.
8. You can not design the future, but you can discover it: test ideas to ditch or develop fast.
9. Never believe you lack resources. Learn lean resourcing, or find more resource.
10. If you take no risk, you will never succeed.

5
THE CULTURAL CODE

Respect for the community

Earn respect

Celebrate to survive

Hamar youth running over a row of bulls' backs as part of his initiation ceremony. The young women fare worse: to show how tough they are they ask to get whipped: this makes them attractive marriage candidates.

Tribes lack the standard tools of corporate control. They do not have reporting systems, schemes of delegation, appraisal systems and internal audit. The age of hyper information and hyper control shows low trust in staff. Instead of data and reports, tribes rely on trust and culture.

Tribal trust comes from everyone signing up to the same rules, habits and beliefs. Those beliefs are instilled in children from the day they are born and are maintained through life with constant peer group pressure. There is no privacy, no hiding place in a tribe: it is obvious when someone is struggling or straying.

The cultural code is a package deal, as it is with all firms. You can not opt in and out of the bits you like or dislike. If you don't like your package deal, you can go elsewhere: tribal people have no choice.

Tribes have cultural habits fit for the 21st century: firms may have to go back to the future to succeed:

Respect for the community, because survival of the group comes before personal interests

Earn respect, because respect comes from what you do and how you are, not from your title

Celebrate to survive: celebrating strengthens bonds which you need when times are hard.

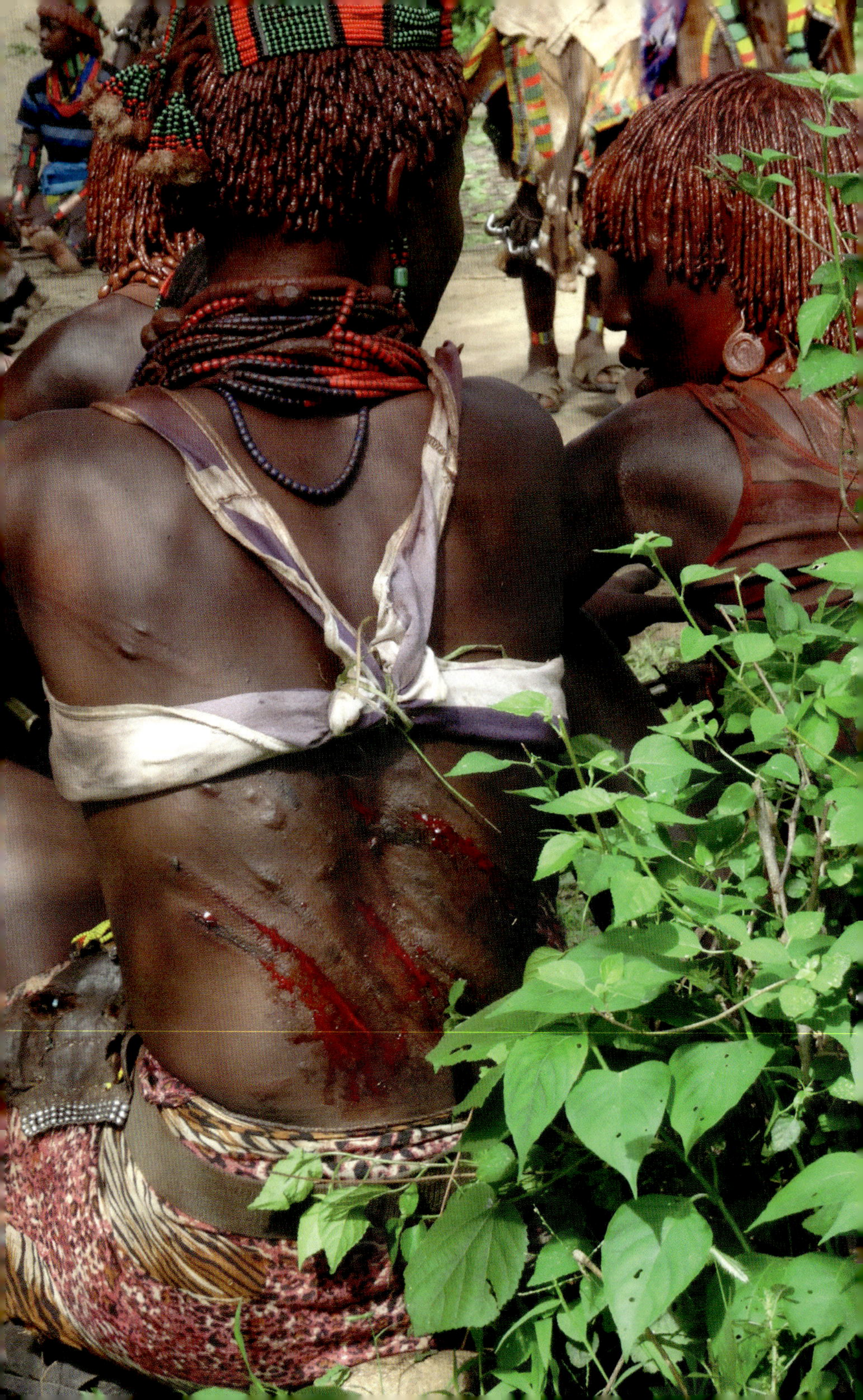

Respect for the community

Respect for the individual is a core value of corporate life. It is an idea which shocks tribal people. To them, that is a recipe for divisiveness, individualism and conflict. They have a much stronger value: respect for the community. Without the community, they cannot survive. They go to great lengths to build commitment to the community, not least in their initiation rites.

The Hamar have a very hard life. To prove their worth, boys have to jump over a line of oxen. The girls have a far harder time. To get married they have to show that they are tough. So while the boys jump the oxen, they ask the men to whip them. The harder they are whipped, the better: it shows how tough they are. And they are meant to keep on chanting while getting whipped.

Perhaps the Hamar girls are lucky: female genital mutilation is still rife in many tribal cultures.

Initiation rites show that the young are ready to become adults. They also show commitment to the community. Any community only survives if everyone buys into its values.

Balance respect for the individual with respect for the community.

(left) Young Hamar females: getting whipped hard shows they are tough, making them attractive marriage candidates.

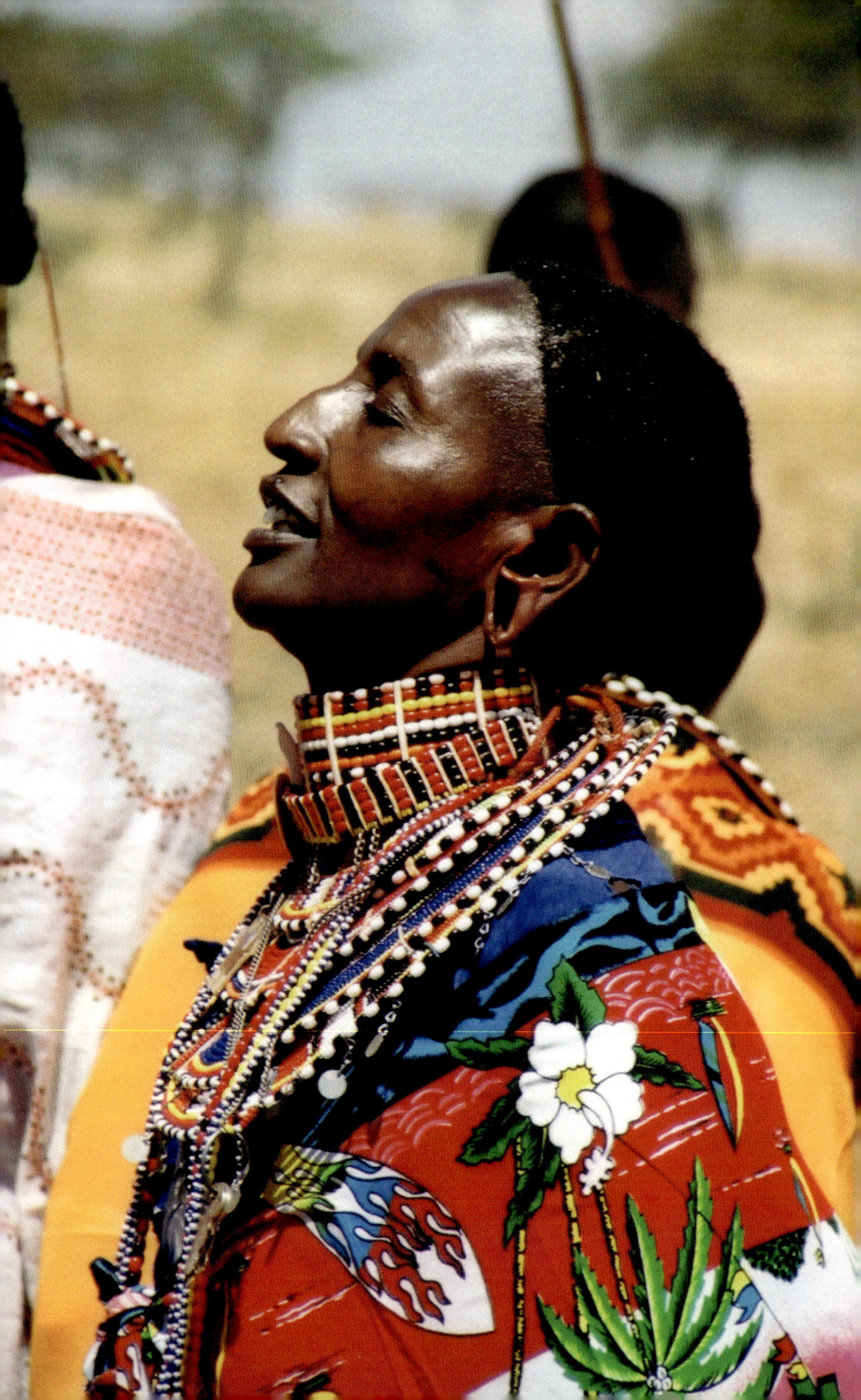

Earn respect

The Fulani elder started on a speech heard through the ages: "the problem with young people is lack of respect". It was not a speech I cared to hear again, but I was obliged to hear it. For once, I was pleased to hear it because this time it was different.

"The first problem is that young people do not respect themselves. Only when they can learn to respect themselves can they start to respect others. When they respect others, they can start to gain respect from other people as well."

"Once they respect themselves and others, and are respected in return; only then can they learn to respect their elders." The elder paused and then chuckled as he added: "if we deserve any respect…"

Respect does not come from your title. You earn respect by what you do and how you are.

(left) Laikipia woman: what they lack in economic capital, they make up for with social capital.

THE TRIBAL CODE

Clockwise from top left: Mursi with lip plate; Konso village with initiation rock and house; Dogon blacksmith who conducts initiations (circumcisions); Hamar painted for initiation.

Earn respect: initiation rites

Hard as I looked, I never found the tribal handbook for new employees. Instead of relying on policies, processes and procedures, tribes have to rely on principles and people. They invest heavily in educating the next generation in the ways of the tribe. Initiation rites mark the moment youth are accepted as full members of the tribe.

Some initiation tests are practical. Konso youth spend months in a separate hall learning about Konso lore and ways before having to lift a stone to show they can manage the hard work.

Mursi girls get their lips cut and put in ever larger lip plates: the larger the lip plate, the more eligible the girl is for marriage.

The Dogon blacksmith takes each cohort of boys up to some rocks where they learn Dogon lore. He then circumcises them, and provided they do not cry out, they get painted and spend the next month naked in the village for all to see that they have now graduated. That would be an interesting initiation for new recruits to a firm.

At least you have the option of choosing a team which fits your values. When you join a team, respect its values.

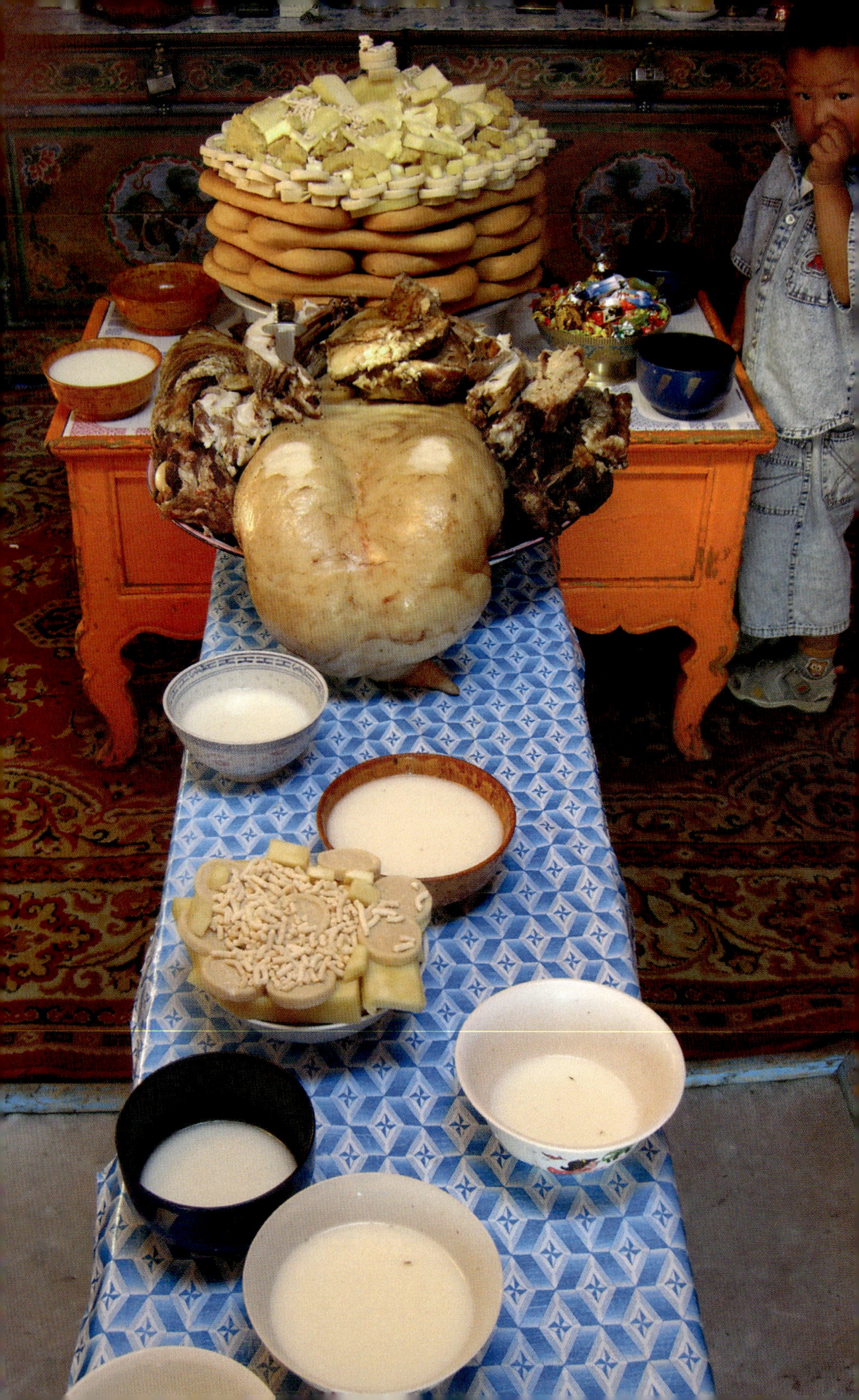

Earn respect: social capital and economic capital

No festival is complete without a feast. Choidog laid on a magnificent feast to celebrate becoming a Living National Treasure (opposite). He gained his award for what he contributed to Mongolia; he celebrated his award by giving some more.

In the arid lands south of the Sahara, the Dogon always want their leader to be rich. As one elder explained: "a rich leader can help us when we have trouble; they can help us with government when we need. A poor leader is no use to us at all."

Traditional societies appreciate the value of economic capital, but they see it as a means to an end, not an end in itself. The ultimate goal is not economic capital, but social capital: the respect of the community matters

Wealth is more agreeable than poverty, but net worth does not equal self-worth.

(left) The feast laid on by Choidog, in his ger, to celebrate becoming a Living National Treasure. Fatty sheep's tail and fermented mare's milk. Enjoy it if you can.

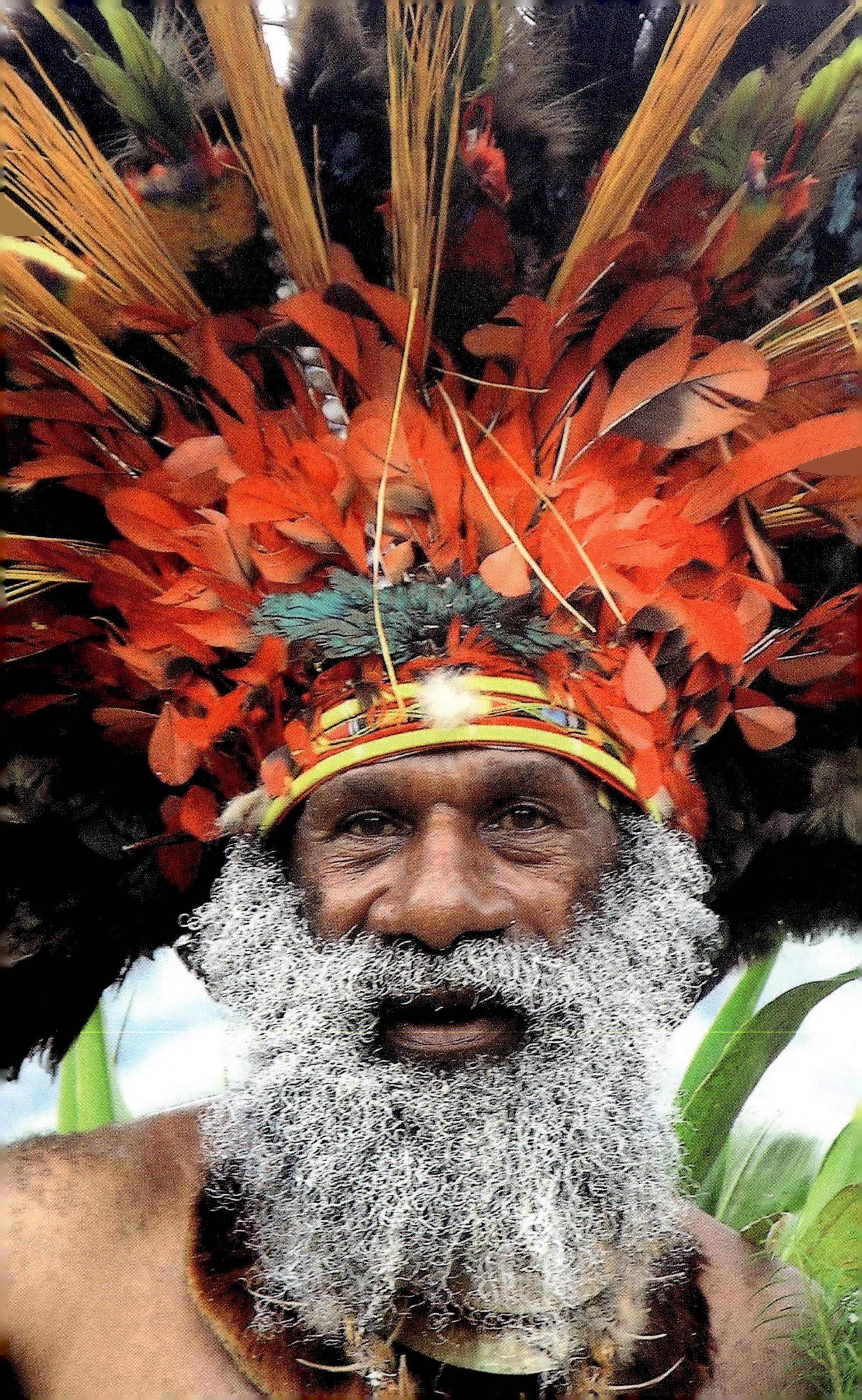

Earn respect: pay and recognition

In his full tribal regalia, everyone can see that Chief John is a Chief with his crown made from bird of paradise feathers. He explained about them: "These feathers show what I can give, not what I can take, for being the chief".

Most of the time, Chief John wore the standard uniform of tribes in Papua New Guinea: second hand clothes from the west. He usually wore a T-shirt with a marijuana plant on the front celebrating the Tijuana Rock Festival of 1992.

His reward for being Chief is not pay, because there is none. His reward is respect and recognition: that is the currency which everyone craves.

As leaders there is often not much you can do about pay. But you can always do more to hand out the feathers of respect and recognition. Low pay may demotivate, but high pay does not motivate for long. If people feel they are respected and recognised for doing a worthwhile job well, they are rarely demotivated.

Chief John, Papua New Guinea

Daily celebrations. Hamar (above), Laikipia (below).

Celebrate to survive

Tribal survival is a collective effort: you cannot survive by yourself. The tribes have found a very good way of building teamwork: they have a party. This is highly effective, and does not appear in most corporate handbooks.

The Laikipia don't have TV, electricity or the internet. In the absence of social media, they have to be social. That means they party. They celebrate pretty much anything: people leaving, people coming, anniversaries, coming of age, and the settlement of a dispute. It is not a good place to be a goat: the goat gets it whenever there is a party and a lucky elder gets to drink the blood from the dying goat's slit throat.

The Laikipia have found the essence of success for global teams, which all have the same problem: how do you trust and manage people you do not see, who work while you sleep and speak a different language? The answer is simple: you party together. Once the human contact and trust is established, the communication flows.

Sales teams celebrate individual success, which is competitive and divisive. High performing teams celebrate collective success. Corporate conferences are not just for pompous executives making dull speeches. They are for people to meet each other and build trust.

To build a team, throw a party. Frequently.

THE TRIBAL CODE

Hamar women dancing and smiling, despite the whipping they ask for and receive during male initiation rites.

The Cultural Code checklist

1. Culture is the glue that holds any team, tribe or firm together.
2. Strong cultures do not exist as values statements: they exist in actions, not in speeches.
3. Earn respect. Respect does not come from your title: it comes from what you do and how you are.
4. Give respect. Respect is a two way street: do not expect to be respected unless you respect others.
5. The team comes first. Respect the community, not just the individual. Individualism drives division and politics.
6. Respect comes from what you give, not from what you take: build social capital as well as economic capital.
7. Culture is a package deal: you can not pick and choose which bits to follow or fight.
8. Sign up to a culture which suits your values.
9. Don't try any tribal initiation rites on your team.
10. Social bonds build trust, so celebrate to survive.

6
THE ANCESTRAL CODE

Appreciate the invisible: the rule of law

Education, education, education

Help from the invisible hand

Enjoy your freedom

Djenne mosque and market (Mali). The visible hand of ancestors (the world's largest mud mosque) and the invisible hand of the market.

Thank you to our ancestors

Adam Smith noted that "Among civilised nations the produce is so great, that a workman, even of the lowest and poorest order, may enjoy greater conveniences of life than it is possible for any savage to acquire." So why should we emulate tribes, when they are poor and we are rich by comparison?

Prosperous societies have inherited advantages which tribes do not have:

- The rule of law
- Education
- Market economy
- Freedom

These advantages have compounded over the last few hundred years. The result is that we benefit from infrastructure we take for granted. Imagine being born into a world without electricity, running water or sewerage, minimal access to any technology, no roads or railways. Poverty would be easy and progress would be hard.

We are rich because of what we have inherited. Much of it is an invisible inheritance, but we can be grateful to our ancestors who laid the foundations of our prosperity.

Unlike many tribes, we do not worship our ancestors. Perhaps we should show more gratitude to them.

THE TRIBAL CODE

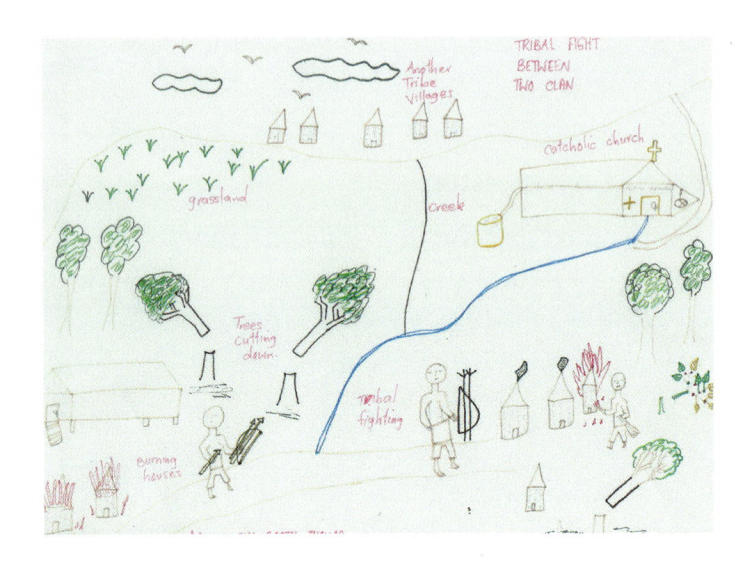

(above) Papua New Guinea: child's violent territory map.

(below) Spot the magistrate, if you can. After the hijack, he wanted tribal justice, not government justice.

Appreciate the invisible: the rule of law

Scene 1: the cowrie shells. Chief John's regalia included cowrie shells, which had high value in the Highlands of Papua New Guinea. Before the colonial era there was no rule of law, so there was no trade, which means no cowrie shells away from the coast. To the tribe, cowrie shells signified wealth, prosperity and the rule of law.

Scene 2: the howls of pain were grating. The Dogon elder explained: "we found a thief from a nearby village. We are making sure he regrets his theft. Should we kill him or hand him over to the police, which means his family will pay money and he will be free tomorrow?"

Scene 3: the child's territory map which showed the effect of tribal rivalry: houses burned down, people killed and crops burned. Those are tough memories for a ten year old to carry.

Scene 4: the magistrate wore second hand clothes and was propping up the bar. He was angry: he had been hijacked on the road. He knew his assailants and would not let them come near his court. He had a better idea "tribal justice: that will sort them out."

We only discover the value of the rule of law when there is none. It is precarious: how long would the rule of law survive in your city if there was no water? Without the rule of law you cannot enforce contracts without a Kalashnikov.

Law is the glue of society and the oil of progress, which tribes do not have.

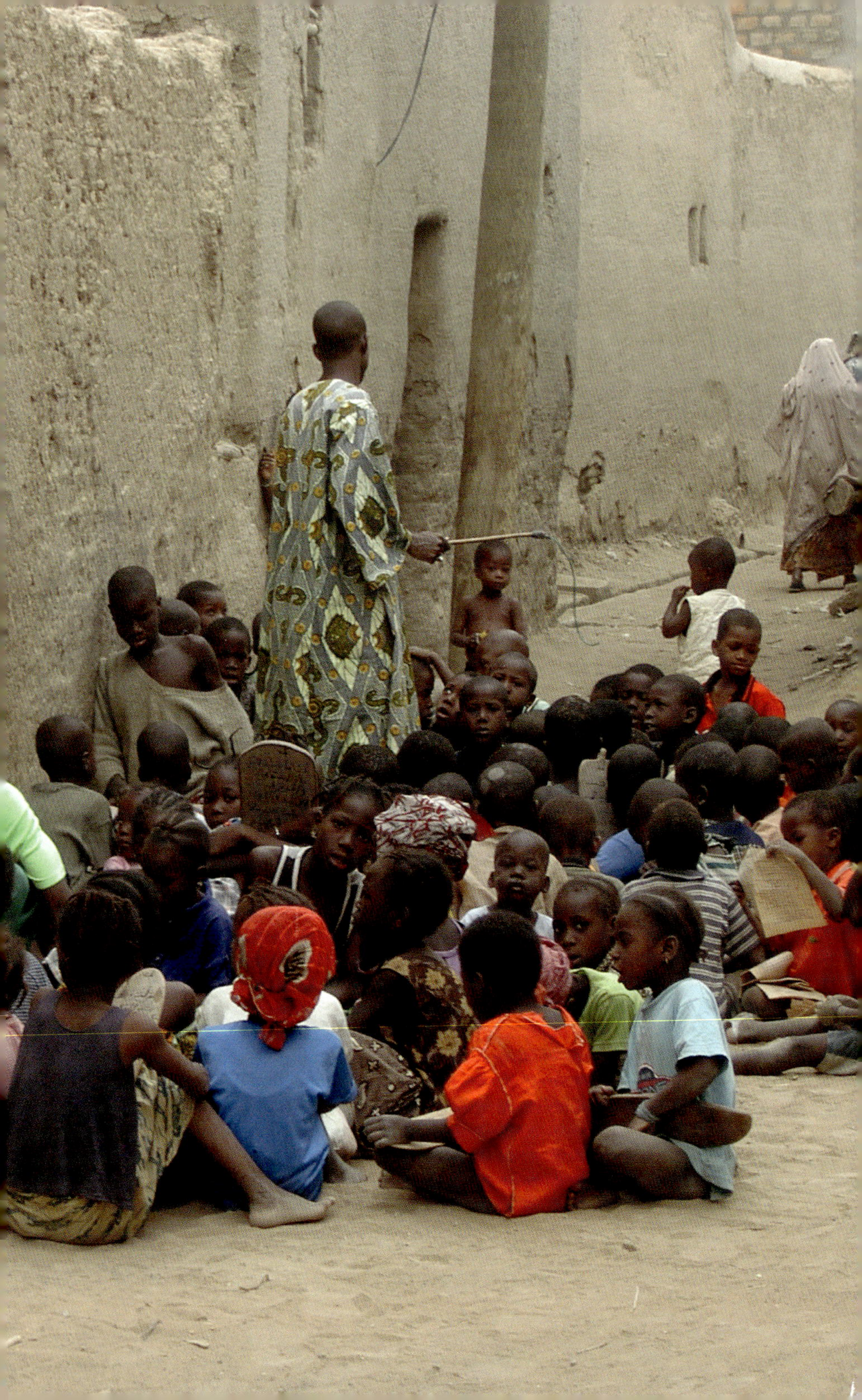

Education, education, education

As a small child, Joseph Nomburi saw a missionary who was clearly very smart: for every question, the missionary consulted his friend: the 'talking paper'. Joseph decided he wanted a friend like that, which meant getting educated. That meant going to a boarding school, a two day trek through hostile territory. Fifty years later, Joseph became Sir Joseph and ambassador to the Imperial Court in Tokyo.

Tribal societies know the value of education and make great sacrifices for it. The Fulani have a simple belief: an educated man never goes hungry. Education is their future.

Tribes make great sacrifices for education. In Timbuktu, school happened in the street, where the teacher's assistant was a whip. For the Laikipia, school was a breeze block building with no doors; others used the shade of tree as an open air school.

The West's great leap in living standards has gone hand in hand with a great leap in education. Many impoverished traditional societies want to follow education's path to prosperity. They have a long way to catch up.

Not everyone enjoys their education, but no education is even worse. Say thank you to your teachers.

(left) A school in Timbuktu. Rote learning and chanting. The teacher's assistant is a whip, in his hand.

Artisans making pins in Djenne, Mali. Adam Smith would be shocked.

Help from the invisible hand

The pin makers were hard at work on the banks of the Niger River in Djenne, Mali. They showed huge expertise in manning small furnaces and turning raw metal into pins. But it was painful to watch: it was highly inefficient.

The pin makers had not read Adam Smith who noted that a skilled artisan working alone might produce 10 pins a day; divide the work among ten semi-skilled workers and they can produce 48,000 pins a day.

We benefit from a market economy marked by deep division of labour, complex supply chains, availability of finance, highly evolved contract and company law. Neither the Djenne pin makers nor most traditional societies have the benefit of the invisible infrastructure of the market economy.

The market economy has deep flaws: greed, inequality and pollution to name a few. But without it, prosperity has to be achieved the medieval way: from conquest loot and plunder, provided you are on the winning side.

Prosperity comes from the helping, but invisible, hand of the market.

THE TRIBAL CODE

Bambara pounding grain, Mali. In good times they need the banking services of the Fulani to save up for the bad times.

The invisible hand: banking on survival

The Fulani are nomadic cattle herders in Mali. Traditionally, they have also been bankers to the community. When the Bambara, the farmers, have a good year they buy some cattle from the Fulani, who continue to look after the stock. In hard times, the Bambara can sell their cattle back to the Fulani and raise some much needed cash.

This arrangement is flawed. When the rains fail, all the farmers suffer and all want to sell: they sell when the price is low and buy when the price is high, in good times. And if the rains fail, then the cattle are likely to die as well.

Banks may also be flawed, but at least your savings will not walk away and die. Banks secure your money (normally) and help the economy grow by lending; insurers provide better cover against disaster than the Fulani can. And the whole infrastructure of property rights, limited liability companies and our legal structure makes economic progress possible.

Whatever you think of bankers, we still need banks.

THE TRIBAL CODE

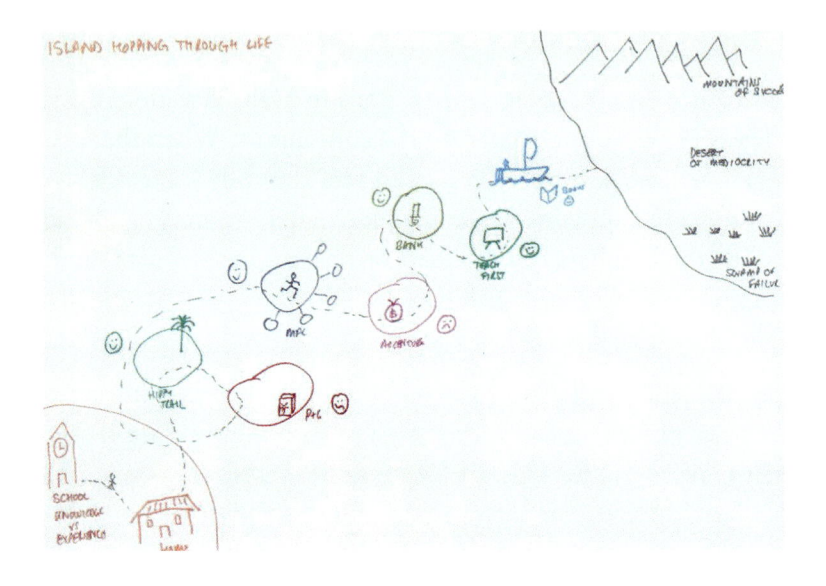

The author's life map: "island hopping through life". Or is that the ultimate tribal sin of tribe hopping?

Enjoy your freedom

Olusu agreed to draw his life map for me. "But" he said "you must draw your life map for me". I was hoisted by my own petard. Without thinking, I quickly drew my life map. It is a sobering experience to draw your whole life on one sheet of paper in fifteen minutes. Try it yourself, now.

I called my map "island hopping through life" as I went from one experience to another. For some people 'career' is a noun; for me it is a verb describing the roller coaster of life.

Olusu looked at my map and went ashen faced with disbelief. "That is not island hopping" he said "that is tribe hopping: no one can hop between tribes!"

We take our freedom for granted. Welfare and savings provides a safety net, and let us have the freedom to island hop through life if we want to. Tribes have no such freedom.

The tribal safety net is their community: without that, they have nothing. They do not have the freedom to hop in and out: they have to commit completely to the tribe.
For this, they endure horrendous initiation rites, complete loss of privacy, and total adherence to tribal rules.

Tribes are better at building social capital than at building economic capital. They have community and a sense of belonging; we have freedom and security. Take your pick.

THE TRIBAL CODE

A Dogon village disappears into the landscape. Try making your living in such a harsh environment.

The ancestral code checklist

1. Our success is built on the backs of our ancestors.
2. The visible hand of the past transforms our lives: electricity, water, transport all make life easier for us.
3. The invisible hand of the market matters: limited liability companies, contract law, banking, insurance and more.
4. The rule of law matters, otherwise the Kalashnikov is king.
5. The rule of law is fragile: mob rule and dictator rule can usurp the law.
6. Education today means prosperity tomorrow.
7. More progress means more specialisation and more skills.
8. It is easy to dislike bankers but hard to live without banking.
9. Freedom to work where we want and for who we want is new and precious.
10. We are lucky inheritors of the visible and invisible foundations of prosperity.

7
YOUR PERSONAL CODE

Build your know-how

Count your blessings

How to wake up in the morning

Know what you want

Tuareg deciphering the code. Or, possibly, looking at photos of themselves taken by the author.

Down the ages, the rich have tried to help the poor, when not exploiting them. The same is true of how we treat tribes. They are easily exploited as supporting cast for a reality TV show, documentary or for some holiday snaps. At other times they are helped by charities, missionaries and agencies who think they know best.

But perhaps we are missing something: maybe tribes can help us. We live in challenging times: tribal people understand all about living in challenging times.

Tribes may hold the key to surviving in a world of AI (Artificial Intelligence). In the long term we will never be smarter than AI, but we will always be more human. Tribal societies have not forgotten what it means to be human.

But even tribal people tire of the hardships they endure. It is when we contrast their struggles with ours, we discover just how lucky we are.

Tribes lack everything from running water and electricity to the joys of social media and cappuccino machines. Despite their evident hardship, they are not miserable. Many find fulfilling lives without any idea of work/life balance, wellbeing coaches and psychologists.

Perhaps they know things which we have forgotten.

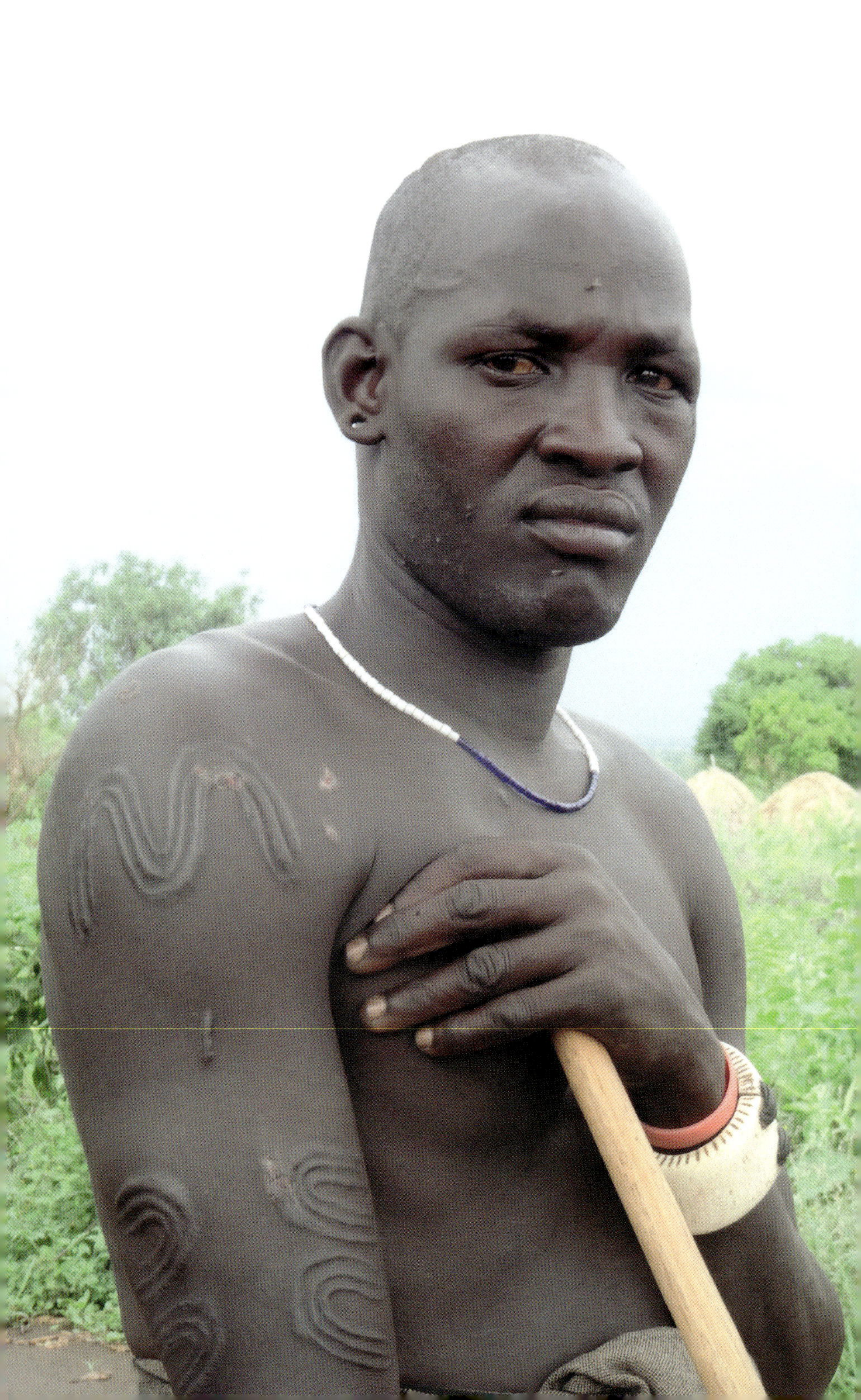

Build your know-how

I asked Chief John who would succeed him as chief. "It will be a democratic decision of the whole village" he said "…and then they will choose my son".

I asked for explanation. "Since he was born, he has seen me deal with all the disputes and characters of the village. He has learned how to deal with everyone, and he is the living repository of every argument I have settled. So of course they have to choose him."

I was nearly converted to Chief John's hereditary principle of democracy: power flows in families, as in America.

The skills required to lead a tribe are the same skills required to lead in an AI world. AI is very good at pattern recognition: if education delivers literate and numerate humans, it delivers no more than second rate computers.

AI cannot deal (yet) with the complexity of human emotions, relations and conflicts; it cannot find creative alternatives and resolve political dog fights. These are the intensely human skills which all tribal leaders learn.

An AI world takes us back to the future: tribal leaders focus on the know-how of dealing with humans.

AI might put you out of a job; know-how can keep you in a job.

(left) Mursi chief, Omo valley.

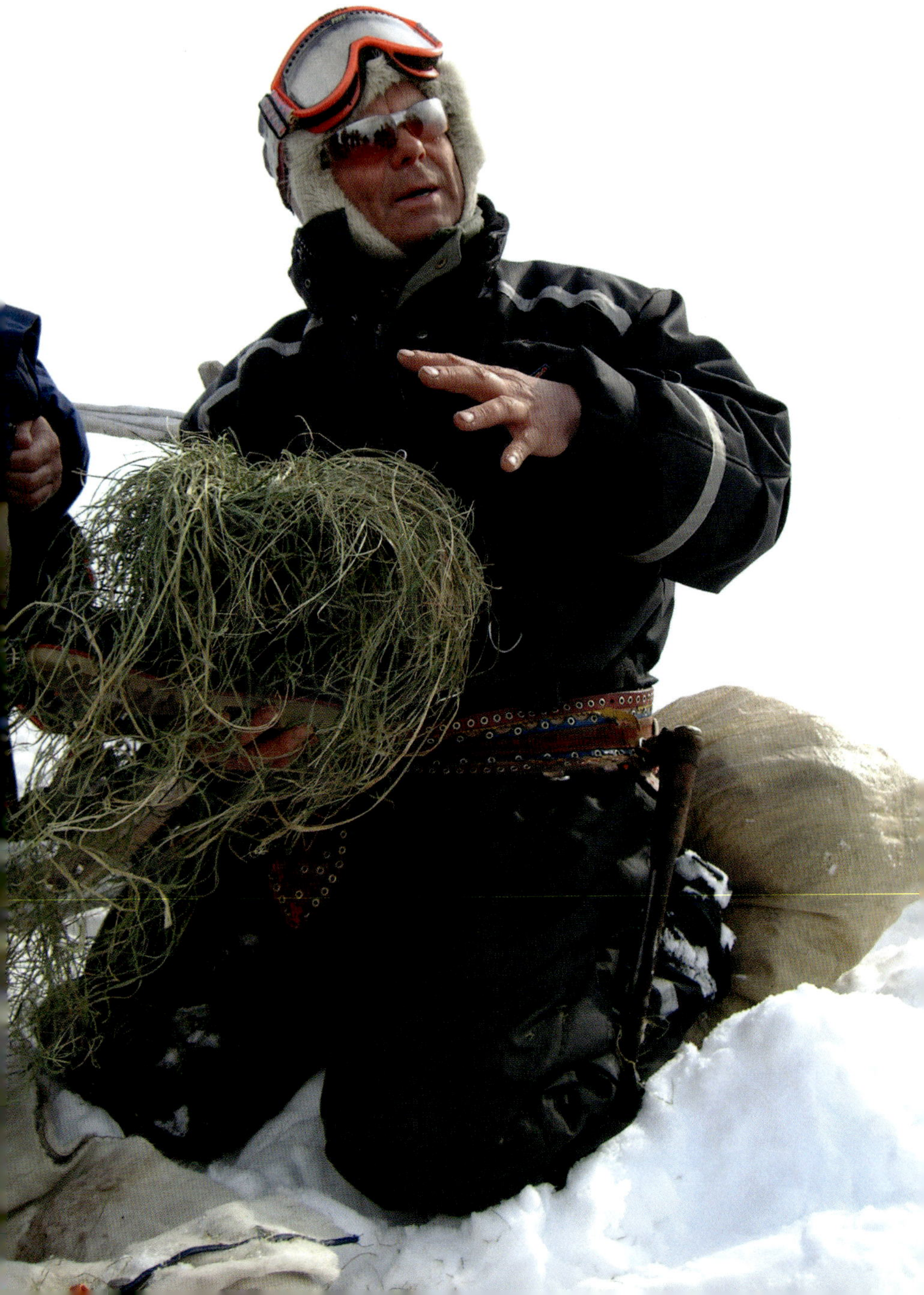

Know-how or freeze

It pays to have the right kit in the Arctic: many layers of the right clothing is a good start. Plastic boots over felt boots are a good combination. The plastic keeps the damp out, and the felt keeps the warmth in.

I discovered that plastic boots not only keep the water out: they keep the water in, if your foot goes through the ice. That is a crisis: a water filled boot quickly becomes a block of ice: say goodbye to your foot. There are not many shoe shops in the middle of the Arctic, so what do you do?

Lars did not panic. He took some dried grass which he had cut in summer, and used that to fashion an inner boot: after a couple of changes, the grass stayed dry and the foot stayed warm. The drama did not become a crisis.

Clearly, if you have access to the internet in the Arctic you can learn survival tricks like this. But by then it is too late: did you remember to pack your carefully cut summer grass with you in the middle of winter? Know-how and experience is the difference between life and death.

At moments of truth, leaders can not resort to the internet to find solutions: you have to draw on your know-how, carefully accumulated from observation and experience.

Learn know-how to survive.

(left) Lars Matthis crafting an Arctic boot. You did remember to bring some dried summer grass with you, didn't you?

Spot the pharmacy (above) and the grocery store (below).
Northern Territory Outback.

Know-how or starve

I was deep in the Outback with some Aborigines. We climbed a rock and admired the view.

"Can you see the grocery store from here?" they asked. All I could see was Outback as far as the eye could see.

"What about the pharmacy?" That was absurd: there were no buildings. So we climbed down and I promptly found myself in the world's largest grocery store and the world's largest pharmacy: the Outback itself.

The Aborigines showed how each plant, bush and tree could be used as food or medicine. I had been like the original Europeans entering the Outback: starving amidst the plenty, much to the puzzlement of the Aborigines.

Survival in any organisation is about knowing what works and what does not work in your context.

THE TRIBAL CODE

Papua New Guinea welcoming party. Learning should always be fun.

Learning know-how

Tribes need an outstanding training and development function: since they cannot select their team members, they have to help everyone be the best of who they are. Many firms help extraordinary people achieve very ordinary things: that is waste which tribes cannot afford.

Most tribes apply highly effective training principles:

Just in time training, which means learning by doing. You cannot learn to ride a horse by reading a book. You have to get in the saddle.

Focus on know-how. Most managers like to focus on know what skills, or technical skills. These are precisely the skills which AI will displace. Know-how skills such as dealing with people is AI-proof and will never go out of fashion.

Consistency and persistence. The training starts from birth, never stops and is consistent throughout. Even I could learn to erect a ger (nomad's tent) after twenty years of practice.

Relevance. Learning how to find food and shelter and how to survive commands attention the way that learning a new IT system does not.

Are you being trained in the right things the right way?

THE TRIBAL CODE

Homes of the Hadza (above) and Fulani (below).

Poverty is not picturesque.

Count your blessings

Media brings the misery of the world to our doorstep every day. And work brings its fair share of pressure, stress and long hours; endless emails, meetings and reporting, and the joy of dealing with difficult colleagues. We have plenty of evidence to tell us that life is not perfect.

But to most tribal people we live in a paradise of fantastical luxury. This baffles them, since we are clearly utterly incompetent at the basic matter of survival: growing food, making utensils, huts and the daily necessities of life.

To see a tribe is to see a different version of reality, which challenges our assumptions about how things are and how they ought to be. It also offers us the chance to be profoundly grateful for things we take for granted, but which tribal societies can scarcely imagine, such as:

Freedom to go where we want and do what we want, within limits

Enjoyment of the basic necessities of life, like water, electricity, housing, health care, education and transport

Security that comes from a welfare state which will save us from complete disaster.

Life may not be perfect, but most tribal people would think we are very, very lucky. Count your blessings.

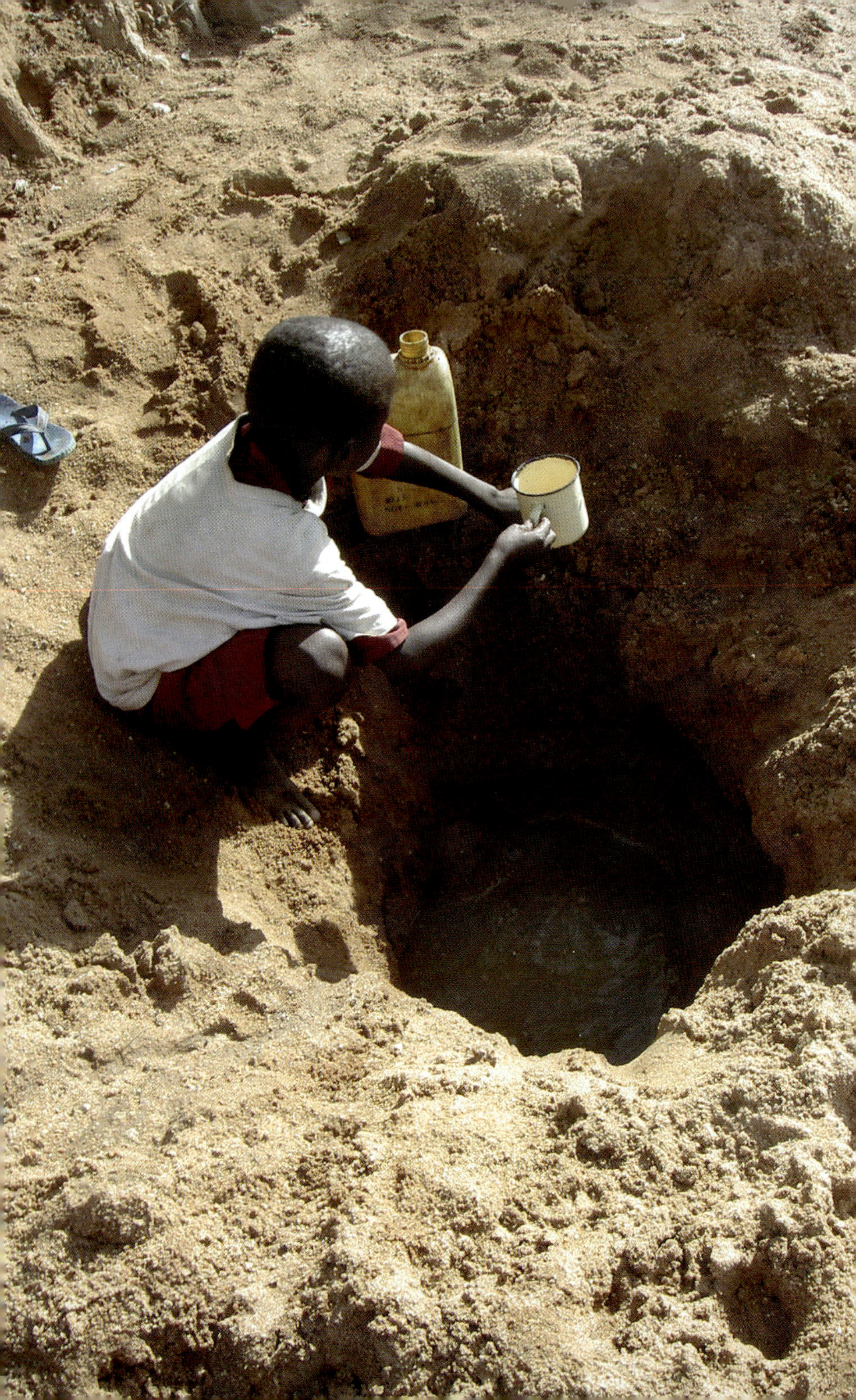

How to wake up in the morning

I had got used to waking up in the morning in the middle of wars, famine, disasters, lying politicians and shifty business people. It was called waking up to the news. It was not a good way to start the day, but still it was far better than the start to many tribal days.

After a hard field trip I got back to civilisation: a hotel with a corrugated iron roof and barbed wire fence. I fell asleep in a filthy bed. The next morning I awoke to a miracle. I went to the bathroom and turned a tap: cold water came out. I did not need to walk 2km to gather water.

A moment later, another miracle: I turned the other tap and warmish water came out. I did not need to gather wood to light a fire and heat the water.

So now I wake up to two miracles in two minutes: hot and cold running water. After that, it is hard to have a bad day, although I succeed occasionally.

It is very easy to ignore the everyday miracles of life: electricity, water, transport, housing and health. We are fortunate to live in an age of relative peace and prosperity.

If you want to turn a bad day into a good day, think of the tribes and count your blessings.

(left) Laikipia boy gathering water from a dry river bed. Never complain about the coffee maker again.

THE TRIBAL CODE

Choimaa, wife of champion horse trainer Choidog, in her ger (tent for living) in Mongolia.

Know what you want

Choimaa's ger was exactly the same as every other ger: door to the south; saddles by the left (west) of the door on the men's side of the ger; cooking utensils to the right (east) of the door on the women's side. As nomads, they live with the bare necessities of life and can move in a day.

I sat where honoured guests sit, drinking their vile fermented mare's milk, freshly milked. At the end of a long discussion I looked round her sparse ger and asked her if there was anything she needed, or anything I could do for her.

She looked astonished. "Why would I need anything?" she asked. "I have my family, friends and health. What more do I need?" She shook her head in disbelief and gave me a toothy smile.

We live in a world where we always want or need more. Choimaa had worked out how to make the hardship of a nomad's journey into a journey she enjoyed.

Whatever your journey is, enjoy it.

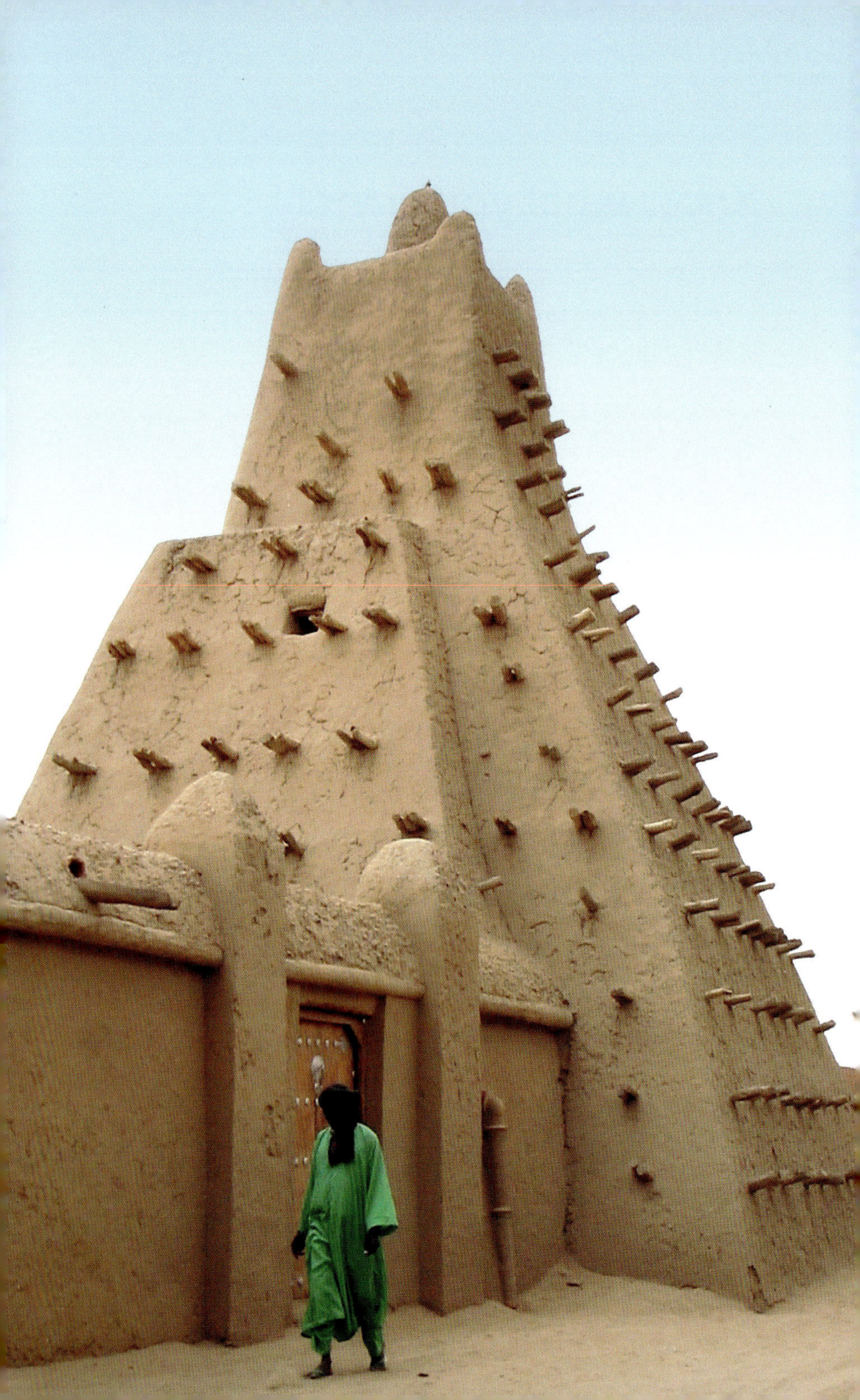

Your personal code: checklist

1. Count your blessings. Would you swap your life for a tribal life?
2. The tribal code is imposed. You can choose your code. Choose well.
3. Unlike tribes, you can find the context which suits your talents and values. Choose your tribe well.
4. AI will replace technical skills. Tribal and human know-how is key to success. Double down on your human talents.
5. Learn what works for you in your context; learn from your experience and your peers.
6. The tribal world keeps changing, your world keeps changing. So keep on learning, keep on adapting.
7. Unlike tribes, your future is not determined for you. You are in control of your destiny.
8. Appreciate what is taken for granted, even hot and cold running water. How bad is life, really?
9. Know what you want and what you need. How much do you really need?
10. Whatever your journey is, enjoy it.

(left) Timbuktu mosque with local Tuareg: the classic traders and raiders of the desert have their own code. What's yours?

THE TRIBAL CODE

(lockwise from top left) Papua New Guinea, Mursi, Kayan (Burma/Thai border) and Tuareg (Mali)

About the book

The Tribal Code is based on original research over 20 years with traditional societies around the world: from Mali to Mongolia, the Arctic to Australia to Papua New Guinea and beyond.

It is also based on working with over 100 of the best, and a few of the worst, organisations on our planet.

The Tribal Code does not claim anthropological integrity. It simply reports what I saw and learned with each tribe while I was there.

I am indebted to all the tribes and firms which have hosted me. I would also like to thank my wife, Hiromi, for her endless support; my thanks also go to Anthony Willoughby for his inspiration. The photos are by the author unless attributed otherwise.

If you have enjoyed the book, I would be hugely grateful if you could post a review of it on Amazon.

Copyright © Jo Owen 2018. All rights reserved.

Published by Auvian Press, an imprint of Auvian plc.
Company registered number: 4853169
ISBN 978-1-9996128-0-1
Design and typesetting by Goldust Design

Author's website: **www.ilead.guru** email: **jo@ilead.guru**

About the author

Jo Owen is a founder of eight NGOs with a combined turnover of over £100 million, including Teach First which is the largest graduate recruiter in the UK. He was a partner at Accenture; he has built businesses in Japan, North America and Europe and he also has started a bank.

He is the only person to win the CMI gold award three times for his books, which include: *Global Teams, How to Lead* and *Mindset of Success.* His books have been published in over 100 editions globally.

He is in demand as a keynote speaker at conferences. Find out more at www.ilead.guru. Email jo@ilead.guru.

The author is the one with no plastic roses on is head.

Photo Anthony Willoughby